Heat, Heart, & Humanity

True Stories: Behind the Sirens

By:
Erik Mendoza

To the men and women who answer the call and carry the weight in the quiet hours, *this is for you.*

Table of Contents

Introduction

This isn't a hero's story. It's the real thing. These are the moments etched into my memory, some for better, some for worse. A few will make you laugh. Others will hit you hard. Every one of them is rooted in truth. These were the calls that shaped me, the laughter that pulled me through, and the heartbreak I carried home, no matter how tough I thought I was.

I've always been drawn to the stories of those who lived through wartime history. I spent years watching documentaries, reading firsthand accounts, and listening to the voices of men and women who saw the worst and lived to tell it. I would never compare myself, or anyone in this profession who isn't a military veteran, to those heroes. But it made me realize something:

We have stories too.

When I first got hired, one of my captains told me, "Start writing it all down. One day, you'll want to remember it." I didn't have the discipline to keep a journal, but the moments that stayed with me, the ones that truly mattered, never left. That's what you'll find in this book.

I'm telling my story because the fire rescue service is filled with incredible people who show up day after day, shift after shift, often without ever feeling seen. This job isn't all sunshine and rainbows. It's dirty. It's brutal. And sometimes, it's thankless. But at its core, it's humbling, a front-row seat to *humanity* at its rawest.

Like I said before, this book is for the men and women who answer the call and carry the weight in the quiet hours. This is for you.

Stay safe,

Erik Mendoza

Chapter 1: The Golden Hour

Every Second Counts.

The tones dropped at 6:30 in the morning, sharp and unforgiving at the tail end of our 24-hour shift.

The red lights in the bunk room lit up like a strobe, jolting me awake in an instant. I've heard that tone a thousand times before, but something in the dispatcher's voice made it hit differently this morning.

"Vehicle versus motorcycle. Person down."

Immediately, I knew it was bad. They don't dispatch that many units for fender-benders. Two fire engines, an EMS Supervisor, a Battalion Chief, and my own unit, Rescue 1, were all tapped for the call. That kind of manpower meant one thing:

We were heading into a dangerous scene.

Calls on the highway are no joke. Fires are dangerous and there's no question about that. But the highway? The highway will kill you faster than any flame. You're working inches from cars flying by at over 70 miles per hour, with drivers distracted, drowsy, or downright reckless. One wrong step, one inattentive driver, and that's it. Guys have always said: *fire might burn you, but the highway will flatten you*, and I'm sure the stats will back that up.

Our crew that morning was tight. James was driving, Mikey in the back. Good guys. Solid.

We jumped out of bed—boots strapped, belts cinched, radios clipped—and out the door.

The moment we hit the road, a burning smell filled the cab. Then the engine light popped on. Was it low coolant? Low oil? Transmission trouble? It didn't matter. For a second, I thought about calling for another rescue to back us up, but we pressed forward.

The call came in for a location just north of a major boulevard, on the northbound lanes of the Turnpike. Here's the thing: on I-95, if a call comes in northbound, north of your position, you usually drop south one exit and loop back around, just in case dispatch got it wrong. That way, if they botched the location, which happens more than it should, you're not stuck rerouting.

But the Turnpike isn't I-95. Unlike I-95, where exits are stacked close together, the Turnpike leaves you stranded if you miss your mark. Overshoot the scene, and you're looking at miles before the next turnaround.

We gambled that dispatch had it right. Traffic seemed to back that up, bumper-to-bumper on the overpass. I radioed in the delay as we pushed ahead.

We rolled up on what looked like a nightmare. A large SUV on top of a small car. This had to be it.

Except it wasn't.

Everyone was out of their vehicles, perfectly fine. Not a single injury. Something felt off, and the Captain agreed. "This isn't it," he said. Moments later, he got word from the Road Ranger already on scene that there was another accident, farther south on the northbound lanes. A motorcycle this time.

The real emergency.

That's when the guilt hit. We had lost precious minutes.

We flipped direction and pushed south.

More delays. More frustration. The clock was ticking.

Then dispatch came over the radio: "Motorcyclist is thought to be 10-7."

Dead.

Silence in the cab. You could feel the weight pressing down on all three of us. James hit the gas. Mikey, in the back, focused in. We weren't giving up.

Mikey double-checked his prep in the back for trauma—IV bags hung, trauma sleeves out, bandages on hand, suction ready. The works. When someone's bleeding out, it's not the time to be looking for gear.

We spotted the Road Ranger's lights on the northbound lanes as we pushed southbound, well beyond the original dispatched location.

We scanned the highway median looking for an opening. Anything. A cut-through. A way to cross safely.

Then we saw him.

Surrounded by cars. *Lying motionless.*

We couldn't wait any longer. It was time to take a calculated risk. We were going to park on the opposite side of the highway instead of continuing to the next exit, which was still miles away. We could reach the patient by crossing over the median.

We coordinated with our two fire engines to create a blockade on the far side of the highway. We had to move fast, but not recklessly.

We jumped out. I sprinted to the median, vaulted over it, and ran straight to the downed rider.

A man, possibly an off-duty firefighter, was already there. He looked at me and said, "He was just awake and breathing, but he's lost consciousness. Breathing is shallow, maybe."

Shallow breathing. Not good.

But not dead either.

My crew arrived with the scoop stretcher, and we moved quickly. A rapid assessment revealed multiple fractures and severe facial trauma. We needed to roll him, but any wrong move could risk spinal damage. Carefully and deliberately, we did, maintaining control the entire time. We secured him and got moving.

I called in the Trauma Alert to the hospital, giving them advance notice of our arrival.

The Golden Hour. That's what we call it. The window after a traumatic injury when a patient's survival odds are at their peak. Past that hour, the odds drop fast. It's why we push like hell. Why seconds matter more than we can afford to waste.

Then we carried him back over the median, dodging traffic as semis thundered past us at 70 miles an hour. The only thing between us and catastrophe were our reflective vests and the strobing lights of the trucks. That rig wasn't just a ride, it was our anchor in the chaos, the last line of safety in a scene that could turn fatal at any second.

We loaded him into the rescue. I jumped in the back. CJ, a solid firefighter from one of the fire engines on scene, slid into the driver's seat.

"You need me to drive?" he asked.

"Get us there," I said.

Inside, we went to work. Mikey cut the rider's clothes off. His vitals were surprisingly stable—shallow breathing, but present.

We needed to get the helmet off quickly to secure his airway, but carefully. James held the neck, and I "jimmied" the helmet off. James, a motorcycle guy, knew the locks and straps. That knowledge made all the difference.

We struggled with the cervical collar. He had a small neck with bad trauma, but we made it work. I checked his mouth. Broken teeth. Removed what we could safely.

We checked lung sounds. Clear. No signs of a pneumothorax, so no needle decompression needed.

He was breathing on his own. But we had the bag-valve-mask ready, just in case. His oxygen levels improved with the non-rebreather mask. We were making progress.

Starting an IV wasn't an option. Almost every limb had an open fracture or severe break. Just below the knee was the only option. James went for the IO, driving it straight into the bone. A modern IO gun squeeze and pop.

We had access.

IO Injection (Intraosseous Access). When veins collapse due to shock or trauma, we don't have time to hunt for IV access. That's where an IO comes in. We drill directly into the patient's bone, usually the tibia or humerus, to deliver fluids and medications fast. Sounds brutal? The idea might, but in reality, it's not. And for patients in cardiac arrest or severe trauma, it's a lifesaving move. The bone marrow acts like a giant vein, absorbing meds and fluids into the bloodstream almost instantly.

Minutes from the Trauma Center.

Seconds mattered.

Then he moved. First his arm, then his head. Our crew locked eyes, and for a split second, hope flooded the box. But we weren't done yet. He still needed the trauma surgeon.

Mikey jumped out as we pulled up to the ER, swinging the back doors open with practiced urgency. We offloaded the young man, turned the stretcher 90 degrees, and rolled him straight into the trauma bay. The trauma team was waiting, fully gowned, focused, and ready. I rattled off the report while they worked fast, moving in sync like a machine.

And just like that, our part was over.

The stretcher was soaked in blood. The box looked like a warzone. But we had done our job. I looked at my guys, these young men who gave everything, and I was proud.

***

Outside the ER, we cleaned the truck, cracked jokes, replayed the scene, and talked about what we could've done better.

Some calls fade. This one won't.

End of shift. No medals. No headlines.

Just another day.

Just another call.

And still, **the best damn job in the world.**

Chapter 2: The First Burn

When I was a kid, like most boys, I had a shortlist of dream jobs: astronaut, fighter pilot, police officer, Jedi, and firefighter. There was always something about helping people and being in the thick of the action that stuck with me.

But for me, it wasn't just a childhood fantasy. There was a specific moment when it became undeniably real.

That moment hit me during a ride-along with one of the busiest fire rescue crews in the country. I was paired with Gus, a firefighter who had no idea he'd end up shaping the course of my life. That day, we ran *three* cardiac arrests back-to-back.

Watching them work—calm under pressure, laser-focused, moving like a machine with a heartbeat—I remember clearly thinking: *This is it. This is what I'm meant to do.* For the first time, I felt it deep in my bones. I didn't just want to ride in the truck. I wanted to be that person, fighting for a stranger's life when every second counts.

That ride-along didn't just open a door. **It lit a fire.**

Right after high school, my best friend Rick and I enrolled in an EMT program. From there, we went straight into basic fire school.

We met people from all walks of life and quickly picked up on the mindset, the culture, and the brotherhood.

But the lingo from the paramedic class was another story. Terms like "DECAP-BTLS" and "hydrogen ions" had my head spinning. I wasn't the most book-smart guy in the room, and when they started firing off medical terms, it felt like they were speaking Martian. I remember thinking, *Blue? Hydrogen? What color am I supposed to be right now?*

But eventually, it clicked. You either sink or swim, and I wasn't about to drown.

The night before my seventh department interview, I faced one of those deep, quiet crossroads in life. Back then, getting hired wasn't easy. Departments were flooded with applicants, and openings were scarce.

At the time, I was working at a cancer treatment center alongside one of the greatest doctors I've ever known, Dr. B. He wasn't only brilliant, but also compassionate. A real mentor.

That night, I went home, prayed hard, and broke down. I asked the Lord, *"If this is where I'm meant to be, open the door. If not, I'll walk away and find another path. But if you give me this shot, I'll give it everything I've got."*

***

The next day was the final interview. It was a three-part process that had led me there. Nerves in full swing, I sat in the waiting room. I wore a freshly pressed suit, and I tried to stay composed. I was waiting for my turn to speak with the fire chief and deputy chief when I saw the door open and the two chiefs step out.

"Mr. Mendoza?" one called.

I immediately stood up—too fast. As I rose, every button on my suit jacket popped off and scattered across the floor.

Time stood still.

My heart sank. I thought, *That's it. I just blew my shot.*

The chief looked down, then back up at me with a grin. "You dropped something, son," he said, laughing. "Come on in, let's start your interview."

"Sir, yes sir," I replied, scrambling to scoop up the buttons and stuff them into my pocket before walking in. The doors closed behind me, and just like that, the interview began.

***

The next day, I was back at the clinic. The interview was still fresh in my mind, every answer and every expression on the chiefs' faces. I tried to stay focused on the job, but underneath it all, I was anxiously and impatiently waiting.

Then my phone rang.

I stepped into the hallway and answered, heart already racing.

"Mr. Mendoza, we'd like to offer you a conditional position with our Fire Rescue Department."

For a moment, I couldn't speak.

I was standing in the middle of the clinic in my scrubs and holding my stethoscope. I laughed. I cried. I probably looked like a maniac to anyone walking by. But I didn't care.

Because in that instant, I knew, *everything was about to change.*

This wasn't just a job offer. It was the start of everything I'd been chasing. Everything I had prayed for.

***

Day one at the fire department's training academy felt like stepping onto a movie set—half excitement, half anxiety, and a whole lot of sweaty palms. Fifteen of us gathered outside the training facility, sizing each other up like contestants on one of my favorite tv shows, *Survivor.*

Who would make it?

Who would break?

We walked into orientation, sat down, and waited. Then the Fire Chief walked in. Tough guy. Impeccably pressed uniform. Quiet stare that could peel paint.

He started speaking, calm at first, almost friendly. I let my guard down. We all did. Then he called on Pauli, one of the recruits. "What's your name, young man?" he asked.

Pauli stood tall. "Hey what's up, my name is Pauli."

And then it exploded.

The Chief lost it. "You will refer to yourself by your LAST NAME ONLY! Every answer will start and end with 'SIR.' Do I make myself clear?!"

"SIR, YES SIR," the classed yelled in unison.

From that moment on, every recruit snapped to attention, even while sitting. Shoulders straight, chins lifted, eyes forward. The tone had officially been set. This wasn't summer camp, **it was going to be hell.**

He marched us outside and ordered us into push-up positions. "Hold it!" he barked. Minutes dragged by like hours. I kept my head up to try to maintain proper posture, and my eyes following him as he spoke.

He leaned in close and screamed, "WHY ARE YOU LOOKING AT ME? LOOK DOWN! YOU HAVE NO RIGHT TO LOOK

AT ME. WE DON'T EVEN KNOW IF YOU'RE GONNA LAST!"

My head snapped down so fast it nearly hit the ground. At that moment, I thought, *This might be it. I might fail out before we even begin.*

But as I glanced around, I saw that everyone wore the same shell-shocked expression. Then it clicked: *The only way out is through.* I stayed locked in, and determined. They could throw whatever they wanted at me.

I wasn't going anywhere.

The training was grueling. Nonstop physical work. Running in bunker gear, fire ground tactics, endless drills, workouts that pushed your limits. It was tough on the body and tougher on the mind.

Everyone struggled, regardless of age or gender. But we bonded over the struggle. We pushed each other, picked each other up, and, yes, took frequent bathroom breaks just to catch our breath.

***

Around the fourth week, we were introduced to something called "the fire can." Imagine an 18-wheeler cargo container, dark red, sealed, and packed with wooden pallets at one end. We filed in wearing full bunker gear and SCBAs, kneeling shoulder-to-shoulder in this metal coffin.

Self-Contained Breathing Apparatus (SCBA). *A portable air cylinder that rests on our back, providing breathable air in hazardous environments.*

Then the fire instructors lit the pallets on fire.

At first, there was only light smoke, but it became thick, swirling, and hot. Then came the flames, dancing above our heads, and crawling across the ceiling like they had minds of their own. The heat pressed down, through our gear and into our bones.

You could hear the pallets crackling and feel the temperature rising every second. Nobody spoke. We just watched and listened. That was the point: to teach us what it felt like, what it looked like, what it sounded like—*to respect it but not fear it.*

Your mind plays tricks on you in there. Even with gear on, the heat is so intense that you feel like you're cooking alive. Knees and ears burning, sweat pouring, lungs tight behind your mask.

But you hold. You have to.

Because this job doesn't let you walk out when it gets uncomfortable. If you're going to run into burning buildings, **then you need to know what hell feels like.**

That day, we all got our first taste.

***

Graduation day was a defining moment. I walked across that stage, and I saw pride in my parents' eyes, I felt the weight of the responsibility that I was about to undertake. At just twenty-one years old, I was stepping into a role where lives would depend on my actions.

While twenty-one might feel young in the medical field, I often remind myself that kids who were barely seventeen years old stormed beaches, flew combat missions, and held trenches in World Wars. Responsibility doesn't wait for the "right" age.

You either rise to meet it or you don't.

That realization reminded me of a line from the 2006 film *The Guardian*, where Kevin Costner's character, Ben Randall, says to his recruits:

"At 24 years old, you have to become that miracle. You have to find a way to be that miracle."

Sure, we're not diving into sub-zero waters off the coast of Alaska, and pulling people from sinking ships. But the weight of that line still holds. In fire rescue, the stakes are real. Someone's worst day becomes your responsibility, and in that moment, *you* have to be that miracle.

That film changed how I saw this job, and showed me clearly what it demands, what it expects, and, most importantly, what it gives back. Brotherhood, purpose, and the chance to truly make a difference.

Chapter 3: Baptism by Fire

The first day at the firehouse wasn't like any other job I've had. I'd worked since I was thirteen in restaurants, painting, and staging companies, but this was different. When you're new on shift, you show up at least an hour early. Nobody tells you to. It's just the unspoken rule for probies. The probationary firefighter who you're relieving is already awake, knocking out morning duties, and hosing down the trucks.

I was assigned to B shift. The guy I relieved happened to be from my academy class. We were both on probation which was a year-long gauntlet of evaluation, judgment, and new challenges.

My assignment: Station 1, Center City, HAZMAT and special ops. This wasn't your average crew. These guys were seasoned, rough around the edges, and heavy smokers with twenty-plus years on the job. They were an older generation and didn't have much patience for probies. All I wanted was to prove that I belonged.

Thankfully, I was assigned to Captain Graves. It was his first day as captain on the fire engine, but he was a veteran of that house. Calm, direct, and steady. He didn't say much, but just enough to make me feel like maybe I could handle it.

What I didn't know then was that we'd become great friends, and that he'd be one of the most important mentors in my life.

The first day was spent cleaning and familiarizing myself with the rig. I learned every compartment, tested equipment, checked air packs, cleaned tools, and studied every inch of that truck. We ran a few minor calls, mostly accidents, but nothing major.

Dinner that night was unforgettable, and not because of the food, but because of the tradition. As the new guy, I was expected to stand in front of the crew and introduce myself, where I was from, why I chose the fire service, something interesting about myself. Then, of course, I had to sing a full-on solo performance in front of seasoned firefighters. Just a rite of passage. Turns out, I wasn't the worst singer. In fact, they made me do it a few more times during probation. To this day, some guys still joke, and ask if I've been working on my "setlist."

The joys of probation.

***

The night began when the tones dropped.

I was sitting in the watch office when the printer's crackling hum sent a jolt through my chest. Dispatch called out ten units.

"Residential structure fire."

The voice was urgent.

I ran the call sheet to the driver's side of the fire engine, slapped it on his seat, and sprinted to my gear. Boots, pants, hood, jacket, helmet—locked in. I jumped into my seat, air pack straps over my shoulders, and before I could process it, we were rolling.

Captain Graves turned in his seat. "We'll be first in for attack."

Lights and sirens blaring. I heard the captain call out a hydrant location that was seventy feet back on the left. He was already preparing for the second-due engine. His calmness steadied me.

What's a Second-Due Engine? In the fire service, every unit responding to a structure fire has a specific assignment based on its order of arrival. The "first-due" engine typically handles fire attack—stretching the initial hose line and making entry. The "second-due" engine, like the one being prepped here, is responsible for a backup line and possibly securing a reliable water supply (depending on the fire department).

As we pulled up, I saw a thin gray stream of smoke curling from the soffit of a small efficiency behind a home. Not thick, but still smoke, and we were first in. I grabbed the jump line (the top fire hose), but it kinked on the pull. The driver yelled out, "Don't worry! Get your tools and rope bag to the front door. I'll get you the nozzle!"

Adrenaline surged. Axe in hand, Captain Graves grabbed the Halligan. **"Top, middle, bottom,"** he nodded toward the door. I swung hard with the butt end of the axe—one hit high, one in the middle, one low—each strike landing like I was chopping into a tree, but with the precision needed to weaken the door's hinges and locks. He drove the Halligan deep into the frame and pried. The door popped.

Smoke rolled out to chest level, and it was thick enough to cloud vision. "Stay low," he instructed, keying his radio. "Engine 1 to Command, making entry with a crew of two, right-hand search pattern, show us as Fire Attack."

We dropped down and crawled inside, navigating through piles of clothes, books, and boxes. Hoarder conditions.

There was talk of a man still inside, and neighbors said his car was there. We had no choice but to keep pushing. Captain Graves was behind me, hand on my shoulder, calling out:

"Fire department! Is anybody inside?"

Then we went silent. *The both of us.*

And in that silence, you could hear it.

That unmistakable crackling of fire. It wasn't just sound. It had texture. A dry, rolling snap and pop, just like back in the burn can at the fire academy. It filled the room like it was alive. *Haunting.*

In the background, the radio buzzed faintly from units checking in and radio traffic stacking on top of itself. My mask hissed with every breath. That was all we could hear, fire, comms, and breathing.

But nothing human.

No voice. No sound of someone needing help.

So… we pushed further.

We found the fire tucked deep in the kitchen, rolling low and angry across the ceiling. The heat hit like a wall, even through our gear. Flames licked across the cabinets and curled down the walls, feeding on everything it touched.

The captain pointed, "Hit that! There too!"

I opened up the nozzle. The stream cut through the smoke with a hard hiss, and steam flashed instantly as it made contact. You could feel the heat start to retreat, pushed back by the pressure and water. The fire didn't die easy, but it backed off like it knew we'd found it.

Other crews were arriving now. They broke windows to ventilate the structure. Visibility began to improve, and eventually, the fire went out.

One of the officers keyed up his radio: "Primary search complete, no victims found. Beginning secondary search."

Primary vs Secondary Search. A "primary search" is fast, focused, and all about life safety. Zero visibility, high heat. You're moving quickly to find victims, not valuables. A "secondary search" comes later, after the fire's under control. It's slower, more thorough, and confirms no one was missed. One is about urgency. The other is about certainty. Both save lives.

At the time, that was true. We hadn't seen anyone inside. Not a sound, not a body. Just smoke, clutter, and heat.

We were celebrating, laughing a little, slapping backs, talking about how good the entry went. It was my first fire, and I felt I belonged.

Then we got the news.

We had been crawling over him the entire time.

The victim was burned beyond recognition. He had taken his own life using accelerants, and hid himself beneath a pile of debris. He was there the whole time, inches beneath our boots, as we advanced the line, tore through smoke, and cleared the room.

None of us saw him until it was over.

That moment hit me hard.

The noise, the adrenaline, and the rush of saving what we could all came to a halt. The energy drained from the scene in an instant. The celebration faded, and there was silence. Not the relieved kind. The reflective kind.

Captain Graves stood nearby and quietly surveyed the scene. After a long pause, he said something I'll never forget:

"We don't create the emergencies. We just respond to them, and do our best to make the situation better."

That line stayed with me and still does.

Because at the end of the day, no matter how chaotic, how tragic, or how heroic the call may be, we're not the story. We're the ones who show up after it begins. And the ones who carry it long after it ends.

And while the flames had been knocked down, the work was far from over.

It was time for overhaul which was arguably harder than the fire itself. Pulling ceilings. Ripping down walls. Tossing furniture. Chasing stubborn hotspots that hide like ghosts in the ashes. The physical work was punishing, but it paled in comparison to the emotional weight of what we had just discovered.

Hotspots? Localized areas within a structure that remain abnormally hot after initial fire suppression.

Captain Graves kept working. So I kept working too.

For the job. For the man buried beneath the debris. For the sobering truth that sometimes we don't get to save them.

***

Back at the truck, we packed hose quietly, until jokes returned. It was their way of resetting. A senior firefighter clapped my back.

"Good job, kid. Welcome to the fire service. You're buying pizza tonight."

That's tradition: first fire, you buy pizza. And so I did. We picked it up from a 24-hour spot, and gathered around the kitchen table.

My first fire.

My first shift.

***

When I woke up the next morning, my relief was already there, and he was nervous, as I'd been. "Do the basics," I told him. "Stay humble. These guys will have your back." Same thing the guy before me said.

As I packed up to go home, Captain Graves pulled me aside. His voice was low and steady.

"Proud of you, kid," he said. "You good?"

I nodded, and this time, it wasn't just out of habit. It was real.

"We did what we could, sir."

And I meant every word. We had given everything we had. No shortcuts. No hesitation. Just hard, honest work in the face of chaos. There wasn't anything glamorous about it, but there was pride. Quiet, steady pride in knowing we showed up and stood tall when it counted.

Graves held my gaze for a beat longer, then gave a small nod of his own. It was the kind of nod that says more than words ever could.

Chapter 4: The Pizza Driver with a Gun

I was a few months into the job, still deep in probation, but finally starting to find my rhythm. We'd just brought on a new probie, Benny, to our shift. Solid guy. One of those people you knew was going places. He'd eventually become one of our Chiefs, but back then, we were just two rookies trying to stay squared away.

Even though he was new, Benny didn't need much coaching. He picked things up quickly. I still showed him the basics. You have to keep the station clean and the trucks ready, but he was a natural. Still, probation means paying your dues. For me, that often meant washing dishes, wiping down counters, and worst of all… making pots of coffee.

Now here's the thing: I hate coffee. I don't drink it. I can't even stand the smell. And yet, somehow, that made me the designated "pot coffee guy". *Every… single… shift.*

One of the veteran firefighters who used to handle the coffee had transferred out. Now, that sacred duty landed on me. And we're not talking regular drip coffee. This was **Cuban coffee**, *café Cubano*, another sacred ritual at the firehouse.

That morning, the lieutenant barked out, "Hey probie, go make coffee for the boys. *Cuban coffee.*"

I had seen it made plenty of times with the moka pot, sugar whip, and the whole routine, but I was done. I wasn't going to be the Cuban coffee guy for the rest of my career.

So I did what any desperate rookie would do,

I sabotaged it.

Let me walk you through Cuban coffee real quick. You use a metal moka pot, fill the bottom with water, pack finely ground espresso in the middle funnel, and screw it shut. You place it on the burner and wait for that strong stream of coffee to start bubbling up.

The magic happens with the *espumita*. You take the first few drops of that liquid gold and mix it with a bunch of sugar to whip up a frothy, caramel-colored syrup. Then, you pour the rest of the coffee over it and stir.

Except, this time, I used salt instead of sugar.

I lined up the cups like a good little probie, poured everyone a shot, and stepped back.

Then they took their first sip.

Almost instantly, the room erupted. Guys were coughing and choking, and one of them even spit coffee through his nose. Some even looked like they had been maced.

"What the hell is this?!"

"You call this coffee?!"

I stayed stone-faced. "Sir, I don't know, sir. I don't even drink pot coffee, sir."

For a moment, I thought I was done. That I had just ended my probation in the worst way possible. But instead, they turned to Benny.

"You know how to make Cuban coffee?"

"Sir, I do," Benny said.

"Good. You're on coffee duty from now on."

"Erik," the lieutenant turned to me, "I don't want to see you around coffee ever again."

"Understood, sir." I said.

And just like that. **Mission Accomplished.**

I gladly went back to cleaning dishes and sweeping floors. Anything was better than making coffee.

***

That evening was quiet. A couple routine medical calls.

By that time in my career, I had transferred over to the rescue unit and was starting to find my groove behind the wheel. I was running lights and sirens, calling intersections, and learning the city like the back of my hand.

Then, right around dinnertime, the tones dropped.

"Shooting. Multiple people involved."

My plate spilled as I jumped up. I ran to the printer, grabbed the run slip, slapped it on the lieutenant's seat, and dove into the back of the rescue. We were rolling within seconds, lights and sirens screaming, weaving through traffic.

Dispatch gave conflicting reports, maybe one victim, maybe more. The lieutenant got on the radio to confirm PD had secured the scene. That's always the rule. You don't walk into chaos without backup.

While we staged, I was in the back prepping. IV bags, trauma shears, tourniquets, and suction. You name it. But the clearance came quickly.

Scene secure. *When a call involves violence, like a shooting, stabbing, or domestic disturbance, fire and EMS don't go straight into the scene. Instead, we stage nearby and wait until police deem it as safe.*

Scene was deemed safe by PD.

We stepped out with gloves on, and bags in hand. You never walk off the rescue empty-handed. I had the trauma bag in one arm, and the LifePak monitor in the other.

A police officer waved us toward a car.

"He's back there."

We turned the corner, and there was a young man lying on the ground. Motionless.

No pulse. No breathing. Multiple gunshot wounds to the head and chest.

Signs clearly incompatible with life.

Nothing to work.

It was the first time I'd ever walked up on a trauma scene and instantly knew that there'd be no CPR. No second chances.

He was already gone.

Just a kid.

And you start wondering, *What happened? Why him? Who was he?*

Then I noticed a man standing by a car, wearing a pizza delivery uniform with a visor, polo, and rubber-soled shoes. He looked stunned, angry, and scared. I heard an officer ask him quietly,

"Is that when he tried to pull you out of the car?"

The driver nodded.

That's when it all clicked.

The kid on the ground had tried to rob the pizza guy. He tried to drag him from his car. He had no idea the driver was armed. The driver grabbed a gun from the center console and fired quickly. Multiple rounds. The would-be robber never had a chance.

You could hear the news choppers overhead. Sirens still echoing like the city hadn't realized it was already *too late*.

We stood there in silence. There was nothing left to do.

The monitor confirmed:

Flatline.

There's a moment on scenes like that where everyone just looks at each other and quietly… *knows*. There's no heroics. No miracle. Just the grim end of a life. One young man dead. Another changed forever.

We packed our gear slowly. No rush. No words. The weight of what had just happened followed us all the way back to the truck.

Because sometimes, this job isn't about saving lives. Sometimes, it's just about showing up, bearing witness, and recognizing that not every call ends in a save.

Some just end.

Chapter 5: The Tracks that Took Her

I had been off of probation for a few years, finally free from the magnifying glass, but far from experienced. By then, I'd seen my fair share of tough calls: some heartbreaking, some bizarre, and a few so ridiculous they had us belly-laughing around the kitchen table.

One minute you're gagging on the smell of human waste (the kind that lingers in your mouth long after you leave). The next, you're laughing until it hurts. But that's the fire service.

At the time, I was still assigned to Center City when whispers of something strange started circulating through the firehouse:

Ebola.

At first, it sounded like a ghost story. Then, like something you'd hear faintly on the news. And before long, it was showing up more and more in HAZMAT meetings.

"What the hell do you mean, Ebola?"

You should've seen our faces. Half disbelief, half dread, all confusion. The internet meme era hadn't fully kicked off yet, but that didn't stop our whiteboards from filling up with crude sketches. Picture firefighters in Tyvek suits battling invisible viruses, scenes straight out of *The Walking Dead: Bunker Edition.*

Firefighters are strange creatures. Sure, we're medics, mechanics, and probably every failed profession rolled into one, but we're also closet comedians and underground cartoonists. So when the captain rolled in with boxes and declared, "We're prepping for a deadly virus, boys," our morbid humor kicked in immediately.

We tore into the boxes like kids on Christmas morning in Chernobyl. Tyvek suits, industrial curtains, respirators, and yellow tape. Stuff we'd seen before, but never in this capacity. We looked like we were about to walk into a nuclear meltdown.

The captain pointed at the spare rescue truck and said, "This is now the designated Ebola truck."

So we turned that thing into a rolling science experiment. We hung curtain rods and taped off sections with thick drapes like we were setting up for Dexter's latest victim. And no, not the cartoon *Dexter's Laboratory.* I'm talking about the live-action one with the serial killer.

Then came the suiting up.

My partner that day was Jay. He was a massive ex-football player who looked like he could bench press the rescue itself. The two of us stuffed ourselves into that truck like overinflated marshmallows.

And that truck? It never rolled. Not once.

It just sat behind the station like a forgotten prop from a disaster movie, slowly turning into a mobile sauna. But it gave us something to laugh about. And in this job, that's worth its weight in gold.

Because, as always, when night falls, *the darkness follows.*

***

Our station sat maybe a quarter-mile from the train tracks. Freight and passenger trains rolled through constantly. It became part of the background noise, like the hum of an old refrigerator. That rhythm was always there, as steady as our own heartbeat.

We were lounging on the couches, half-watching a movie, when the tones sliced through the comfort.

"Train versus pedestrian."

We made our way to the rescue, moving quickly but controlled, with lights on and sirens cutting through the night.

As we approached the intersection, traffic was already backing up. The crossing arms were down, and the Amtrak train sat motionless with twelve passenger cars stretched across the tracks and packed with people.

People heading home, now frozen, silent witnesses to something they'd never forget.

The scene was bathed in ghostly white from the train's own lights. Beneath the bogie, there was nothing but shadows. The speed walk to the train felt like the slowest walk I'd ever taken. Every step was thick with dread, like wading through molasses.

I couldn't hear them, but I could see their faces pressed against the glass, staring at us, frozen in time.

You could feel the weight of it in the air. People shaken to their core, even if they weren't physically touched. You don't forget that kind of look.

Or that kind of silence.

We were the transport unit, and by the time we arrived, other crews were already working. We grabbed the equipment we needed and moved quickly, heading straight for the tracks.

I saw her as crews pulled her from under the train. *Or what was left of her.* Everyone grabbed a limb, whatever we could reach. I remember the weight.

Heavy like a sandbag.

Her body was destroyed. Shredded. A massive gash across her neck. Limbs torn, hardly held together by strands of skin and ligaments. But she was alive. *Barely.*

She was… crying.

Not screaming. Not calling out. Just crying.

Silent tears streamed down her face as blood, dirt, and sweat mixed all together. She was conscious enough to know she was dying.

That wrecked me.

Because no matter how much training you've had, nothing prepares you for the moment when someone's body is destroyed—**but their spirit hasn't let go yet.**

Her body was coming undone in real time.

Every movement, every bump of the stretcher, felt like it could be the one to finish what the train had started. We weren't just fighting time. We were fighting physics.

We got her into the rescue and fought to save her life.

Intubation was impossible. Her throat was torn open. We resorted to a modified breathing technique, tried to get IV access, but with her body in pieces, it was a nightmare.

Blood everywhere.

We were working in chaos.

The golden hour didn't matter here. This wasn't a rescue. *It was just time slipping away.*

And not but thirty seconds later, she lost her pulse. We started CPR, racing to the hospital. But we knew that we were essentially delivering a body to the ER.

At the hospital, after just a few minutes of trying, the doctor gave the order, "Stop all resuscitation efforts."

And just like that, it was done.

***

Back at the truck, we cleaned up in silence. Blood, skin, and fragments of a life that we couldn't save. Everything felt heavier than before. Then a police officer stepped in and filled in the blanks.

It was suicide.

But not the kind you typically picture. Not quick or impulsive. This was different. The train had just picked up passengers and was only beginning to roll out of the station. It was moving so slowly, it hadn't even had the chance to pick up speed.

She waited calmly until it crept just far enough past the platform. Then she stepped forward. The train didn't sever her clean. It tore her apart... slowly, piece by piece.

Not enough force to kill her instantly. *Just enough to make sure that there was no going back.*

***

Later that night, we sat together for a stress debrief. Call it CISD. Call it a vent session. Call it whatever you want, they matter.

We sat together and processed it the best we could.

Up to that point, it was the worst call I'd ever experienced. And the only thing that helped was what the seasoned guys would continue to say: "We don't create these emergencies. We just show up and try to make things better."

We didn't cause the pain.

We just tried to stop the bleeding both literally and emotionally.

But you learn quickly that if you let these things sit too long, they'll fester.

So you talk.

You share.

Then you let it go.

At least enough to keep moving forward.

Chapter 6: The Tree That Didn't Let Go

Every shift starts the same way.

We show up at 7 a.m. at the station, but we line up at 8 a.m. sharp. During probation, we would show up an hour early, but after we passed, we'd come in 30 to 45 minutes early. Just enough time to relieve your guy, go over the prior shift, and get a handle on the day ahead. Lineup was part roll call, part family meeting. We'd check the rigs, talk about training, map out the day, and most importantly, figure out what was on the menu.

That day, our designated cook was a rookie driver, Nico.

Army vet. Former NYPD. Full-time beatboxer.

He was one of those guys who'd already lived a whole life before the fire service. And over time, he became one of my closest friends. Nico's got a big heart and an even smarter mouth. He'll break his back to help you, and then roast you without mercy five minutes later if you step out of line.

That morning, he was trying to push quinoa on the guys like it was steak and potatoes. They weren't having it.

"Quinoa? Kenya what? Give us rice and beans!"

Classic Nico.

Back then, eating healthy just wasn't a firehouse thing. But he was a leader, afraid of no one, and one of the first to fight the good fight, the battle against the firehouse gut. A fight I'm still losing, one fat roll at a time.

My boy, Louie, was there too. Smart as hell, hilarious, and quick on the draw (both on calls and with comebacks). The kind of medic who would throw a precordial thump like a gorilla and not even flinch.

You know, he actually did that once. Hit a guy so hard in the chest, it looked like he was trying to knock him into next week.

Precordial Thump. A single, forceful strike to the center of a patient's chest, specifically over the sternum, used in rare emergency cases to try to convert a witnessed, pulseless ventricular tachycardia (VT) or ventricular fibrillation (VF) into a perfusing rhythm.

That specific thump didn't bring the guy back, but it bought us a few seconds. We jumped in—CPR, meds, intubation—and gave him everything we had. And yeah, we saved him in the end. But it all started with Louie and that thump.

He was that kind of guy. Chaotic, but in the best way.

Then there was my wedding. Louie was a groomsman.

He showed up late, of course. He came flying in with one shoe on, practically sliding out of the car. His girlfriend was still inside of it.

Instead of helping her out, he jumped out, and he yelled, "It was her fault, not mine!" while waving a wad of cash wrapped in a Ziploc bag.

It looked like a scene straight out of the movie *Casino*, when Sharon Stone storms out of the car and the camera cuts back and forth.

He wasn't late. He was on Cuban time.

I couldn't stop laughing. You just have to love this guy. But he made it. Just in time to hop on the bus with us to the ceremony.

That's Louie for you. Loud. Messy. A walking hurricane. But always there when it matters. See, this job becomes your life. Your crew becomes your family. You share shifts, holidays, victories, and heartbreaks.

And on one particular shift, we were about to share one of the worst.

***

The sky was a dull gray. Not stormy, not bright. Just heavy. That kind of air where nothing feels loud, even when it is.

Then the call dropped:

"Hanging in the park."

At that moment, I had never been to a hanging before. My mind started racing, trying to picture it ahead of time and preparing for the worst, just to soften the blow.

One of my mentors, and one of my best friends both on the job and in the surf, Dano once told me, "The most important thing on any scene is to stay cool. If you stay cool, everyone else will too."

And he was right. Panic spreads faster than fire.

As we rolled lights and sirens through traffic, it started to drizzle. Just enough to hear it, a light tapping on the windshield. The wipers groaned back and forth. The dashboard rattled like something loose inside was trying to crawl out. It was just the old rescue truck doing what it always did, and for a while, those were the only sounds.

Louie and I sat in silence. He focused on driving while the lieutenant prepped for arrival. We waited for whatever came next.

We turned onto the block just as the fire engine arrived ahead of us. The captain made first contact and keyed up the radio:

"Obvious Signal 7."

Now, for a captain to call it that fast, it had to be unmistakable. We don't throw that code around lightly. Usually, you check vitals, run through the motions, confirm there's truly nothing to be done. But when someone calls it *obvious* over the radio? That means what they're seeing isn't survivable, that person is dead—no doubt about it.

Still, we walked over. You always do.

We stepped out of the rescue and crossed the grass toward the scene.

It was Halloween. The one day of the year when death is supposed to be pretend. Plastic pumpkins and spiderwebs hung from fences. Skeleton decorations rocked in the breeze.

A kid in a costume walked by with a parent, oblivious to what was happening just a few yards away. The whole scene felt staged. But it was real.

Too real.

And, there it was.

A massive oak tree, like something straight out of a horror film. Gnarled branches. Thick roots. Situated in the middle of a small, beat-up neighborhood park—old swings, a rusty slide, cracked sidewalks.

Not the kind of park you'd see on a brochure.

But still, *a kids' park.*

And from that tree hung a woman. Maybe mid-fifties. Brown manila rope wrapped tight around her neck.

But what hit me the hardest, what still shakes me, was her knees.

They were on the ground. Not hovering. Just resting. Like she had knelt there by choice. No overturned chair. No step stool. Nothing. She could've just stood up. She could've lived.

But she didn't.

You have to understand, your body doesn't want to die.

You can try to drown yourself, but your brain will force your body up for air. The survival instinct is baked into our DNA. It's automatic. Hanging is brutal because it fights against that instinct.

You choke, your legs kick, your lungs beg for air. But she had fought all of that. She stayed still. She let it happen. That's how much she wanted to go.

That's the part that destroyed me.

She had chosen a place meant for children, laughter, swings, and scraped knees. But now, it was tainted. A playground turned into a *graveyard.*

Her injuries were clearly incompatible with life, and we had no choice but to declare her deceased. There was nothing left to do, but we stood there for a moment anyway, just absorbing it all.

The rain was still falling lightly, steady, and unbothered. The park was silent and empty in a way that felt deliberate. It felt like the end of a movie where the audience doesn't get closure, but only the credit lines.

I've seen other hangings since. But nothing like that. Not because of gore. Not because of lack of chaos. Not even because of choice.

It was something deeper and something that stuck with me in ways I still can't fully explain.

***

Not long after that hanging, I bought my first house, only to find a massive oak tree standing in the front yard. Same size. Same twisted limbs. Same haunting silhouette as the one in that park.

A few days after moving in, I had it cut down. The neighbors were furious. One woman even cried. "It was beautiful," she said. "You should've never done that."

But they'll never know why.

They'll never know the *tree* I saw that day.

And they'll never understand the *silence it left behind.*

Chapter 7: The Cinnamon Challenge

A few years after probation, I was deep into studying for the Driver Engineer's exam. It was one of the most competitive tests in our department. Everyone wanted off of the rescue truck. It was mentally and physically exhausting.

At the time, we were considered one of the busiest departments in the nation, based on raw call volume per rescue unit. Our top rescues were blowing past five thousand calls a year. That kind of pace didn't just wear you out. It buried you. Most guys just wanted a break. Even a temporary escape from the burnout.

So we studied. Hard. We were eight months out, and my study group was locked in. We studied everywhere. Houses, libraries, the fire stations, it didn't matter. Pushed each other. Respected each other. Never slacked. Eventually, other guys wanted in our group because we were structured, focused, and relentless.

It was serious business.

Truthfully though, by then, I'd grown comfortable on the rescue. It was where the consistent action was, and I felt effective there. But my captain at the time, Ray, always reminded me: "If you're going to stay on the box, you might as well get paid for it. Get promoted."

The next logical step was Lieutenant. And to get there, you first had to become a driver on the fire truck.

***

I was at Center City working with Ant, one of the guys I got hired with and someone who'd eventually become one of my best friends. Solid firefighter. Excellent medic. Calm under pressure. Ant never let anything rattle him. He was always the one keeping the temperature down when things got hot.

That day, things were slow, until one of the senior guys decided to shake up the monotony with a classic firehouse stunt:

The Cinnamon Challenge.

Simple enough in theory: swallow a palmful of ground cinnamon without coughing, choking, or exploding like a cartoon character.

What they don't tell you is that cinnamon immediately dries out every molecule of moisture in your mouth and throat. It triggers violent coughing fits, and swallowing a handful feels like inhaling powdered lava.

Ant and I lined up with cinnamon in hand. We tossed it back at the same time and immediately regretted every life decision that led us to that moment.

I coughed so hard a cinnamon cloud exploded out of my nose and mouth, filling the kitchen like a smoke machine at a bad concert.

My eyes watered. My throat burned. I gagged like I was being pepper sprayed.

Ant didn't do much better. He got some of it down, which just made him gag in silence. We looked absolutely ridiculous.

And that's when the tones dropped.

"Overdose. Gas station."

We locked eyes and shifted from firehouse nonsense to reality in an instant. Still coughing, we bolted for the rescue. I jumped behind the wheel, cinnamon dust still coating my tongue. Ant hopped in the back. Andy, the lieutenant, climbed into the passenger seat. It was just another routine overdose. We rolled Code 3 through traffic.

Code 3. An emergency response using lights and sirens, indicating the highest urgency when responding to calls.

Sirens wailed. Lights flashed. Ant was still choking in the back. I was driving like I didn't just inhale a spice rack. We arrived at the gas station. The air outside was thick with gasoline fumes, which did not pair well with the lingering taste of cinnamon.

Inside, the clerk looked panicked. "He won't open the door!" he shouted and pointed toward the restroom.

The old wooden door hung slightly ajar with its rusted hinges barely holding on. We approached slowly. Each step echoed with the weight of what might be waiting on the other side.

In our line of work, there's a well-known rule: *Try before you pry.*

So, we tried the door.

Locked.

Time to pry—the fun part.

Andy was focused. "Grab the irons. Let's pop this door." Ant grabbed the Halligan. I took the axe. A few solid swings, and we partially forced the door. The patient had collapsed behind it, and he was blocking the full opening. Ant, being slightly thinner, squeezed through the crack and gently dragged him out.

The Irons. *The combination of a flat-head axe and a Halligan bar that are married together as a single forcible entry set of tools.*

Young guy in his early thirties. Pinpoint pupils. Shallow breaths. A needle still dangled from his arm. Heroin, most likely laced with fentanyl (the kind that's hard to reverse).

We got right to work. Ant immediately began rescue breathing with the bag-valve-mask, perfectly timing his breaths to the patient's shallow respirations and pushing precious oxygen back into his brain.

If the brain goes more than four to six minutes without sufficient oxygen, irreversible damage begins. Ant knew exactly how crucial each breath was.

Meanwhile, I moved quickly to establish IV access. I placed the saline lock on the patient's chest, wrapped the tourniquet around his arm, flicked the vein to bring it up, and wiped it clean with an alcohol swab. With steady precision, I slid the 18-gauge needle into his vein, felt the familiar pop, and watched blood surge into the chamber.

Smooth entry.

I locked the IV securely and prepared the Narcan.

Narcan. *Rapidly reverses opioid overdoses by blocking opioid receptors, essentially bringing someone back from the brink of death.*

Usually, one or two milligrams does the trick.

But not today.

Ant kept breathing for the patient as we administered dose after dose, still with no reaction.

We didn't give up.

Ultimately, we administered a substantial dosage to bring him back. Ant noticed first, calling out, "He's breathing stronger." The patient's breaths became deeper, and his chest began to rise and fall visibly. Just a few moments later, the patient's eyelids began to flutter, and his eyes watered slightly as consciousness slowly returned.

His breathing quickened, and suddenly, he shot upright with eyes full of panic and confusion.

His gaze darted around the room, frightened and disoriented. "What…what happened?" he managed to whisper.

Ant's voice was calm. "You overdosed, buddy."

The guy blinked. "I don't do drugs."

Ant gestured to the needle we'd pulled from his arm. "This was in your vein, man."

"Oh… shit," he muttered.

I reassured him, "You're not in trouble. But we've got to take you in. We gave you a lot of Narcan."

He nodded slowly, quiet, and grateful. In that moment, he wasn't a drug user to us. He was just a person who needed help.

That's something this job teaches you: **addiction doesn't define someone's worth.**

As we loaded him onto the stretcher, I finally took a good look at Ant. He was still covered in cinnamon powder. His face was red, sweaty, and swollen. It was on his uniform, in his hair, and even dusted across his boots.

Andy looked at us and cracked up. "Man, rough one for you boys, huh?"

I managed a weak laugh. "Yeah, you could say that."

We all chuckled, the tension finally starting to ease. Moments like that, where the humor cuts through the turmoil, are what keep you grounded in this job.

It was another save, and another reminder of why we do what we do. We cleaned up, regrouped, and headed back to the station. We were grateful for the good outcome, even if we'd nearly choked ourselves half to death on cinnamon beforehand.

Some days at the firehouse are intense and emotional.

Other days are just absurdly funny.

And sometimes, like today, they're both.

Chapter 8: The Strap, and the Muddle

It was just after 6 a.m. when the tones dropped:

"Seizure call."

Pretty routine in our world. You'll run a seizure or two per shift, but nothing that really makes your heart rate spike.

We pulled up to an apartment complex on the southeast side of town and headed upstairs. The guy was in his fifties, shirtless, barefoot, and shredded. Not bodybuilder shredded. More like retired Navy SEAL shredded. Lean muscle, tough skin, and a look like he could throw a punch even while unconscious.

He was postictal, which is the foggy, confused state most patients enter after a seizure. The lieutenant drew up Versed, just in case another seizure hit and we needed to calm things down again.

We got the patient onto the stretcher, secured him, and made our way down the elevator. So far, so good.

> *Versed and seizures.* A fast-acting benzodiazepine used to stop active seizures or to prevent them from recurring. It's a go-to for paramedics because it works quickly, can be used in chaotic environments, and doesn't require a complex setup.

But en route to the hospital, everything changed.

I was in the driver's seat of the cab, seatbelt on, just about to pull out of the apartment complex when I heard the lieutenant yell from the back, "Stop the truck! Get back here—now!"

I slammed the brake, threw it in park, and ran to the rear doors. When I flung them open, it was absolute chaos.

Jen, our firefighter in the back, was getting her hair yanked by our Navy SEAL look-alike. The lieutenant was wrestling the patient, trying to keep the man's other arm from swinging at her.

The patient was awake. Partially naked. Fully enraged.

Yes, you heard that right.

Right hand on his junk, left arm writhing against the restraint while still tugging Jen's hair. I didn't hesitate. I launched myself into the back of the truck like I was going up for a dunk in the NBA Finals, one shoulder straight into his chest.

He didn't budge.

This guy had superhuman strength. I've wrestled violent psych patients, people who have overdosed, and drunks, all in self-defense. But this was different. He tossed us around like rag dolls.

The lieutenant shouted for help on the radio. "Code 3. We need PD here, and FAST!"

And then it got worse.

He reached down. Not for a weapon, but for his backside, where feces, yes **feces**, was freely oozing out. And then, like something out of a horror show, he grabbed it, smeared it, and tried to throw it.

We were in a 6x12 metal box. No escape. Just three of us in there with a naked, poop-slinging, adrenaline-fueled rage machine.

Seconds felt like hours.

Jen broke free and drew up the Haldol. She jammed it into his shoulder, but nothing happened.

Nothing!

Haldol. *A powerful antipsychotic used in emergency medicine to sedate violent or combative patients.*

He kept going like it was adrenaline in its purest form. I was holding his legs. The lieutenant was holding his arms. Jen had his head. And still, we were losing.

That's when Jen made her move, and she quickly snaked an arm around the man's shoulders to keep him from thrashing side to side.

Ten seconds. Maybe fifteen.

I ran for the syringe, drew up a bit more of Haldol, and drove it into his shoulder.

He blinked. His eyes glazed, and his arms fell limp. His breathing relaxed. He fell asleep.

We all just stood there, covered in blood, sweat, and God knows what else, breathing hard and staring at each other like:

"What the hell just happened?!"

We reconnected the LifePak. His vitals were perfect and his heart rate was solid with oxygen at 100%. No major trauma. Just trauma to *us*.

Jen drew up and administered the Benadryl, which is a requirement when Haldol is given to prevent dystonic reactions.

Just minutes after our distress call, the back doors swung open. The cops stood there with their eyes wide and black gloves on.

"What can we do?" one of them asked.

Dystonic Reactions from Haldol. *An involuntary muscle contraction, often sudden and severe.*

We were catching our breath, and our uniforms were soaked in various bodily fluids, the aftermath literally clinging to everything. "It's handled," the lieutenant said, shaking his head and laughing.

"But damn… that was wild."

***

When we arrived at the ER, one of the cops looked at our guy and said: "Oh yeah… we know him. Good guy. Won multiple competitions for his sheer strength. But he's been hit in the head a few too many times. Took a bat to the skull not long ago."

Well … that explains it.

He probably left out the part where he was ex–Special Forces or something… but hey, what do I know?

Back at the station, we scrubbed everything in the truck, including the floors, cabinets, walls. But the worst part? My radio strap. That thing was soaked. Blood. Sweat. Feces. It was like a biohazard braid. I tossed it into the decon bin and never looked back.

Nothing like wrapping up a shift with a call that feels like a UFC match in a porta potty.

And you wonder why we drink beer like it's holy water.

Chapter 9: The Broth Disaster

We had just wrapped up a hazmat drill, and I was back at the station. I still was a firefighter, early in my career, and very much the rookie.

Happy, the senior driver at the station was in charge of chow that day. He was making a giant pot of chicken soup, and as you'll see in later chapters, I'm not exactly famous for my cooking skills. I can hold my own with a burger or slap together a decent "Chipotal" wrap (yes, Chipotal, you'll get the full story in Chapter 15), but anything beyond that? Let's just say nobody's lining up to eat my cooking.

While Happy was off getting fuel for his truck, he called me and said, "Hey Dozer, drain the chicken for me."

Now, I had no idea what that meant. *Drain the chicken? What exactly was I draining here? Did I hear him right?*

But I was the rookie at the fire house, and Happy was Happy. You don't question it, you just do it.

So I walked into the kitchen like a good soldier, found the biggest strainer I could, and poured that entire pot of hot chicken soup, that liquid gold, right into it. *All the broth drained straight down the sink.*

I was left staring at a pile of sad, wet chicken pieces in a dry pot. It looked like wrinkly skin after a long bath, just sitting there, both confused and defeated. That's when I knew.

I messed up... big.

I called over to Ker, one of the other drivers, who was lounging on the couch with his feet up and watching football.

"Hey Ker," I said, "I think I messed up, messed up bad."

He walked into the kitchen, took one look at the pot, and his face went pale.

"What the hell did you do?! You poured out the broth?! The soup's supposed to be ready in 30 minutes!" he yelled, his southern accent thick and unmistakable.

I had that classic *"what did I just do?"* face going.

"Well," he said, "we need to fix this."

And Ker, bless him, decided we were going to rebuild the broth from scratch.

Now keep in mind, we had nothing to work with. No bouillon cubes, no stock or broth, and no more fresh chicken. Just faucet water, some dusty chicken powder from the back of the locker, and sheer desperation.

We tried to reboil it, to season it, and to salvage something resembling flavor, but it tasted like a crime against poultry. And then… Happy walked in.

"How's the soup?"

I opened my mouth to confess, but before I could speak, Ker sold me out faster than a probie skipping dish duty.

"Mendoza dumped the broth," he blurted. "Poured it right down the sink."

Happy looked at me like I'd just kicked his dog.

"What were you thinking?!" he barked.

"I obviously wasn't thinking, Happy," I said.

Happy yelled, "I told you to drain the pasta—not dump the whole soup!"

"Ohhhhh," I groaned.

"That's it. You're out of the kitchen!" he snapped.

But… it was too late.

The boys were already lining up for lunch. They started dishing up bowls of whatever Frankenstein soup we had created, tasting it, grimacing, and shooting looks around like, *Who did this?*

And I just sat there, silently… taking the well-deserved hits. And there were many.

That moment was the beginning of a long trail of evidence proving just how bad I am at cooking. This book might be filled with stories of life, death, and everything in between, but it could just as easily be titled, *How I Suck at Cooking*.

And that day?

That day was Exhibit A.

Chapter 10: The Jaws

It was just after noon when the call dropped:

"Vehicle versus tree."

We were assigned first as the extrication team. And the second I heard *vehicle versus tree*, I knew it wasn't going to be good. Trees don't move. They've been here longer than most of us have been alive. Their roots run deep, like generational trauma, and when you hit one, it's usually the soft body that breaks first.

> *Extrication Team. In vehicular accidents where victims are trapped inside, an extrication team is responsible for removing them safely and quickly. They operate specialized tools (commonly known as the Jaws of Life from Hurst), including hydraulic cutters, spreaders, and rams, to peel open twisted metal and to create access points. Their job isn't just one of brute force, but also surgical precision.*

We rolled out with sirens in a too-sunny afternoon, and we arrived at the scene on a quiet residential street. No traffic. No crowd. Just one mangled car wrapped around an ancient oak tree. That tree stood tall and green, heavy moss swaying like it hadn't noticed the object crumpled at its base.

The front of the car was folded like an accordion. One young man was partially-hanging out of the windshield. His torso was limp, and his legs were pinned under the car's dash. The other person was still inside the vehicle on the passenger side, but it was completely crushed around him. Neither person moved. But we could see that both were breathing—shallow.

We chalked the wheels first. Basic safety. The last thing you want is a car shifting while you're buried waist-deep inside it.

The Heavy Rescue equipment truck showed up right behind us. The gas-powered hydraulic system kicked on with a roar. Pumps whining. Valves clacking. The smell of fuel thick in the air. It's a mechanic's symphony, and we were the orchestra.

I was assigned to the spreaders, which is my favorite job on calls like this.

I unrolled the hose, clipped in the hydraulic line, and gave it a test squeeze. The pressure held. The spreaders are simple, yet savage. They are two steel arms powered by raw force and capable of splitting metal like it's tin foil. You don't fight it. You guide it. Let it do what it was built to do.

The captain quickly came to call angles and direct cuts. The teamwork was tight, clean, and efficient. There were no wasted motions.

While we worked the metal, the other medics worked the people. One firefighter climbed into the car from the back just to reach the passenger. Only the firefighter's upper torso and a single arm could fit through the opening, but it was enough. The young man in the passenger seat may have been shallowly breathing, but even just reassuring him, whether he could hear it or not, meant everything.

Another firefighter climbed onto the hood to stabilize the driver. His skin was pale, and his lips were beginning to turn white. He was still breathing, but not well. His airway needed to be secured.

Out of the corner of my eye, I caught the firefighter using the laryngoscope and slipping in the ET tube for the driver. Probably the hardest tube insertion I've ever seen.

Intubation. When a patient can't breathe on their own, or looks like they're about to stop breathing, we intubate. That means placing a tube down the trachea so we can take over their breathing. It takes precision and a steady hand, especially when you're doing it on the hood of a wrecked car, surrounded by broken glass, blood, and the ticking of time.

I was back on the tool. My spreaders couldn't get a bite. The door was crumpled inward, pinned tight against the frame, and the hinges fused in place like welded steel. I pried and wedged, trying to force a gap, but the metal just flexed.

Without missing a beat, Louie stepped in with the cutters.

The car clanked with that unmistakable sound—*chk-chk-chk*—as the blades locked onto the thick hinge bolts. Then came the high-pitched whine of hydraulic pressure, building like a scream, followed by a sharp *pop!* as the steel finally gave. One bolt. Then another. Then the last.

The resistance lessened, but the door was still tight, still fighting us.

I stepped in again, jammed the spreader tips into the seam, and leaned in. Pressure built with every twist of the handle. The metal groaned—deep, angry, and low. You could feel the vibration crawl up through your boots.

Then... *crack!*

The whole door shifted outward.

But as soon as we opened the door, it was clear that we weren't done.

The steering column had collapsed into the driver's lap, and it was pinning his legs beneath the dash. He was wedged awkwardly in place with part of his body inside the car and part sprawled onto the hood. His pelvis and both femurs were likely shattered, and every second trapped under that twisted metal meant more bleeding we couldn't control.

"We need the ram." The captain ordered.

Lobo already was ahead of the captain, dragging the hydraulic ram out of the compartment. He braced it between the crushed dash and the solid frame rail of the driver's side, angling the cylinder just right to avoid shifting the entire dashboard further into his legs.

"Set... ram extending," Lobo said.

The tool hissed to life.

You could hear the metal creaking, rivets popping, and bolts protesting under the pressure as the ram extended. It sounded like something out of a submarine with the kind of noise that you'd expect as the hull starts to give way under pressure.

Slowly, the dash began to lift. The steering column peeled away from the driver's legs, inch by inch. It was the kind of movement you barely notice in the moment, but it feels massive when it means that someone gets to keep their legs or *their life*.

The driver gasped as the weight released and air rushed back into his lungs, and his face contorted from both the pain and the relief. Still, he remained unresponsive and intubated.

"You're doing good," the medic said, hand firm on the drivers shoulder.

"Almost there. Just stay with me—we've got you."

Talking to them doesn't just reassure the patient; it also reassures us. It doesn't matter if we know they can hear us or not. There's something powerful about speaking to someone who's barely hanging on. It's our way of telling them... *we're still here*, still fighting for you.

And believe it or not, there have been reports of unresponsive patients later recalling the voices of their rescuers.

Once we had enough clearance, the medics slid the backboard in behind the driver and began stabilizing him.

No panic. No wasted breath. Just grit, steel, and execution.

But the second patient was worse off. The car's passenger side was completely caved in. We couldn't get to him from his own door. I crawled across the shattered console and over the seat, and I started peeling metal from around his legs. It smelled like antifreeze, blood, and burnt plastic. I moved quickly but carefully because every inch mattered. My gloves were slick. Arms burning from the weight of the Jaws.

But we got him free.

We slid the backboard in at an angle.

"Hold C-spine," someone said. We froze. He was stabilized. We moved as one. The passenger came out, still breathing but shallowly, and he was out cold.

Both patients were now out and loaded onto stretchers, and each were placed into separate rescues. Both tagged as Level 1 Trauma Alerts with life-threatening injuries and no room for error. Every second mattered. Time had started to bleed into the golden hour's most precious minutes, but we still were inside the window.

We stood and watched as the rescues disappeared into traffic, and they headed for the trauma center. The scene was cleared. The chaos had quieted. That part was done.

We stood in the road for a minute with tools scattered and sirens fading. That oak hadn't moved a single inch. It never does. But the lives that slammed into it? Changed forever.

Calls like this stick with you, not just because of the gore or the chaos, but because of how fast everything can flip. One second you're driving home from a party. The next, your car is wrapped around a tree, and strangers are cutting you out of it.

We packed up the tools. Rolled the hose. Went over what we could have done better. We reflect after every call so that we don't make the same mistakes twice. You can always be better.

Just another call. Another life held together with bandages and a prayer.

Another day borrowed from fate.

Chapter 11: Close Enough to Touch

At the Special Ops station, training wasn't optional—it was life insurance.

Every morning, without fail, we hit the ropes. High-point anchors. Mechanical advantage systems. Belay setups. Rescue haul systems. Pick-off maneuvers. Some mornings, we strung ropes from the dining room table to the kitchen just to practice tensioning. On other mornings, we stretched lines across the bay to simulate confined space entries or edge transitions.

And it wasn't just rope work. That massive heavy rescue truck sitting in the bay was packed with every tool and piece of equipment you could imagine: Hurst tools; cribbing sets; airbags; meters; and all kinds of specialty gear.

We trained because when the tones dropped, there was no time to flip through an instruction manual. You had to lean into the unknown. Because one day, when it was your crew hanging over the edge or crawling through the wreckage, you'd need every skill to be sharp and second nature.

There's no room for "good enough" in this line of work. You're either ready, or you're not ready.

That morning, the tones dropped:

"High-angle rescue on the beach. Scaffold failure. Painter is dangling."

We climbed into the truck quickly, lights blaring, sirens screaming, and tires humming under the weight of adrenaline. The ten-minute ride felt like thirty minutes.

As we raced toward the coast, the captain turned to me.

"You're going up, kid."

My mouth went dry. Every drill I'd ever run came flooding back all at once. I thought about anchor points, harness checks, pick-off straps, edge guards, haul lines, and escape plans. This wasn't a scenario anymore.

This was real.

As we neared the beach, the radio crackled: "Tower Ladder 2 on scene. We've got a painter that is hanging from a suspended scaffold at approximately 85 feet above the ground. We'll be raising the ladder to make the grab."

The plan was to have the operator on the platform truck grab the stranded painter, and I would act as backup in case the attempt was unsuccessful or a second was needed.

The announced plan sounded confident, like they had it under control. But I knew better. At that height, with the wind off the ocean and time slipping away, anything could go wrong.

Platform Truck (Tower Ladder): Instead of an open ladder, a platform truck has a bucket or "basket" mounted at the tip of the aerial. It's bulkier and takes slightly longer to set up, but offers a stable, enclosed space for rescues, hose operations, or elevated master streams. Think of it as a mobile balcony or a cherry picker.

Still, I stayed focused and ready for anything.

***

The moment we arrived on scene, I moved fast.

I stepped into the harness and cinched it tight at the hips until it bit into my skin, double-checking everything for good measure. Carabiners were locked and clipped high on my chest with anchor straps secured to my belt. I had the rope bag ready to sling over my shoulder, my helmet snug with the chin strap clipped, and my gloves tucked into place – all ready to deploy the moment they were needed.

It was mechanical, and my hands moved faster than my brain could process what was happening. But beneath it all, the weight of the situation was very heavy:

If I screw this up, someone dies.

The beach was chaos. Cops directing traffic. Tourists staring from the sidewalk. Ocean wind whipping salt into the air. The building loomed above us with its glass and steel stretching into a bright, cloudless sky. The ladder truck had taken a gamble and angled across Beach Road and behind the parallel-parked cars, facing perpendicular to the two building towers.

Not ideal positioning.

The space between the two towers was close to 100 feet wide.

I saw the target. The painter dangled from a broken scaffold. He was just a tiny figure swaying 85 feet up, with a rope wrapped around his harness and attached to the twisted, leaning scaffold.

And then… a sight that made my stomach drop.

A second painter lay on the ground, but covered with a white sheet.

Dead.

The realization hit me like a gut punch. One dead. One hanging. No time for emotions now, but they were in the back of my mind.

The ladder driver made his move. I watched, heart pounding in my ears, as he extended the aerial across the gap and far beyond what seemed reasonable. The bucket man crept out using the hand controls, steady and deliberate, and he was careful not to strike the stranded man or anything around him. The operator braced against the whipping ocean wind, balancing with every shift of the platform.

Then… contact!

He tied off the painter, freed him from the failed lift, and secured him inside the bucket. Inch by inch, agonizingly slow, they began to head back towards safety.

A full-body shudder of relief hit me when the platform touched down. You couldn't script it better. No rope deployment. No mid-air pick-off. No roll-the-dice gamble with someone's life hanging by a carabiner.

Those ladder boys were absolute studs that day. They were veterans who knew exactly what they were doing, even under that intense pressure.

I unbuckled my gear with shaking hands. Harness off. Ropes packed neatly back into their bags. Carabiners stacked and stowed. The adrenaline dump made my knees feel like jelly.

We didn't get the glory that day. And honestly? Thank God. The goal was always to save the victim, and not to put on a show.

***

The ride back to the station felt like getting let out of school early. Windows down. Ocean air rushing through the cabin. Disney World might've gotten canceled, but somebody's dad got to go home that day.

And that? That was better than any fairy tale.

But I never forgot the other man.

The one we couldn't save.

He was out there doing his job, just like all of us do every day.

Chapter 12: In His Head

The call dropped late at night:

"Suicide on the highway."

Someone had walked straight into traffic. No hesitation. No second-guessing. Just raw finality.

We were assigned from the north side of the city. I slid into my boots with my mind racing. *Were we going to find him still breathing, or just be scooping body parts off the asphalt?*

As we got onto the highway, brake lights shimmered ahead of us— a growing sea of red just past the overpass. We slowed down and weaved carefully through traffic until we spotted a cluster of cars stopped awkwardly across the lanes. They weren't blocking traffic so much as shielding the body from getting hit again.

We angled the rescue truck to cover the scene and threw on our traffic vests. Then we went out the doors and hustled toward him under the harsh glare of a dozen headlights.

He was intact and had a pulse. His arms, legs, and head were still there. That was the first blessing.

I immediately told the lieutenant, "I'll get C-spine!," which means I'd stabilize the man's neck and head so no further damage could be done to his spine if he was somehow still hanging on.

I gloved up, knelt down, and carefully slid my hands beneath his skull.

And that's when it happened.

My right hand sank straight into his head.

Not a wound.

It was a crater.

A soft, horrific depression where bone should've been. Three of my fingers pressed right into his brain.

I jerked my hand back instinctively, fighting every urge to pull away and freak out, but I kept my left hand firm and stabilized his neck. Panic beat against my chest like a drum.

"LT—his skull is crushed in!" I choked out.

He didn't flinch.

"No problem. Get the collar on and roll him over. Let's go."

And that's what we did.

I reset myself, forced the fear down, and held the man's head straight while we log-rolled him onto a backboard. The cervical collar snapped into place, locking his neck so that it was motionless. Then, he was onto the stretcher and into the truck. Doors slammed shut behind us. Lights and sirens to the ER.

He was still breathing.

Still had a pulse.

But for how long?

In the back of the rescue, we worked fast. We started two large-bore IVs, one jammed into each arm. One of the firefighters bagged him with oxygen, which assisted with ventilations. I grabbed the blood pressure cuff to wrap it around his arm. As I lifted his right arm to slip the cuff underneath, the truck swerved—just enough.

His limp elbow, hanging open like a broken hinge with bones exposed, suddenly snapped shut with surprising forc**e. It trapped my fingers in the joint like a sprung mousetrap.** The same fingers that, moments earlier, had touched his exposed brain matter. I yanked my hand free and flexed my fingers in disbelief, but again shoved my feelings aside.

We had work to do.

There was blood everywhere. Avulsions, lacerations, and holes that we couldn't even fully see. It was like trying to plug a sinking ship with duct tape.

We worked quickly with trauma dressings, pressure wraps, and splints. But then his oxygen levels started tanking, and his chest wasn't rising evenly. One side of his chest was barely moving, and his blood pressure was dropping. Fast.

Tension pneumothorax.

I grabbed a 14-gauge decompression needle and found the landmark, which was the second intercostal space, mid-clavicular line, just above the third rib to avoid the neurovascular bundle. I plunged the needle into the chest wall.

__Needle Decompression:__ When a lung collapses, usually from trauma, it can leak air into the space between the lung and chest wall. That trapped air builds pressure, crushing the lung and pushing the heart sideways. If that pressure is not relieved, it's fatal. A decompression needle is a thick, hollow catheter that punches through the chest wall, releasing the pressure like a punctured balloon. It's brutal, but it works. If you've ever seen the most recent Mission Impossible movie, then you know what I'm talking about.

There was a hiss of escaping air, just like popping a tire. The chest began to rise again.

But just moments after we stabilized his airway, he lost a pulse and went into cardiac arrest. Without hesitation, we started CPR with hard and fast compressions driving into his chest as the LifePak charged. The monitor confirmed a witnessed, shockable rhythm.

"Charging to 360 joules," the lieutenant called out.

The LifePak whined, and its pitch rose as it built power. Our crew moved instinctively, with all hands off the man. The lieutenant scanned the area with a sharp glance to make sure no one was touching the patient.

"Head clear. Chest clear. Legs clear," he said, his voice steady.

His thumb pressed the shock button, and the patient's body reacted in an instant. A violent jolt snapped through him. His chest arched, and his arms twitched. His feet recoiled against the stretcher. The current surged from pad to pad, ripping through muscle, nerve, and heart tissue like a lightning strike trying to bring order to chaos.

Shocking the Truth! *In the movies, they shock everything. Flatline? Shock it. Agonal breaths? Shock it. Someone collapses dramatically in the ER? Paddle slam, full jolt, and suddenly they're awake and talking.*

But real life doesn't work that way.

In reality, there are only a few heart rhythms that can actually be shocked, and these are chaotic or dangerously fast heart rhythms where a defibrillator can deliver a synchronized bolt of energy to reset the heart and give it a chance to restart correctly. That's why, in the field, we're often doing chest compressions for minutes, or even longer, and waiting for one of two things: a shockable rhythm to develop; or a pulse to return. It's not fast or dramatic, but it's real.

We immediately resumed compressions. Two straight minutes of deep, rhythmic pressure followed. Sweat ran down my back. Every chest pump was a plea for his heart to come back online.

Then came a flicker. A pulse. Weak, but there.

He was back—*for now.*

We pushed the next line of meds to keep his pressure up and to prevent him from slipping back into cardiac arrest. It wasn't over, but we'd bought him time.

Despite everything, he still had a weak pulse when we rolled through the hospital bay doors.

The surgeons were already waiting. Their eyes scanned him, and their hands were ready. They got him onto their trauma table without hesitation.

"We still have a pulse," the lieutenant said firmly. "Multiple vehicle impacts. Suspected suicide attempt. Severe head trauma."

The doctors listened and moved into action.

They slammed chest tubes into both sides of his rib cage. Blood poured from those tubes like a fountain. Compared to those tubes, the decompression needles that we had placed en route to the hospital felt like nothing more than Band-Aids. The internal bleeding was massive and seemingly unstoppable.

Chest Tube. A thick rubber hose inserted into the chest cavity to drain blood or air.

Still, the doctors fought. Just like us.

You never stop trying. Not until the monitor flatlines for good.

We stepped back with bloodied hands and drained bodies, watching in silence as the hospital team carried on the fight.

Maybe he had minutes.

Maybe only seconds.

But in that moment, he wasn't alone. People were doing everything they could to save him. Despite the circumstances. Despite the fact that he had tried to end his own life, he was surrounded by strangers who cared enough to fight for it.

And even if no one else remembers who stood by him in those final moments, *we always will.*

Chapter 13: Another Day at the Latrine

Some calls, you can hear before you even arrive. This was one of those calls. The tones dropped:

"Natural gas leak. Construction site."

A large gas pipe burst violently. It wasn't even in our city. But under our mutual aid agreement, if you had the HAZMAT sticker on your helmet, you rolled out. No questions asked.

Every HAZMAT call needs at least two teams on scene (one to work, one to back the first team up). On that day, the problem was that the first team was already tied up. That made us the first team by default.

As we came down the street, we could already hear it. A sharp, high-pitched hiss cut through the wind. It sounded like a thousand angry snakes. The closer we got, the louder it *hisssssed*. You could feel it vibrating in your chest.

Big line. Big problem.

We parked the trucks with the wind at our backs—always park upwind. Last thing you want is to charge headfirst into an invisible cloud of gas. We hit the pavement fast and bunked out in seconds. It was showtime.

The captain came hustling back after his 360, and his face was already serious under the brim of his helmet.

360 Size-Up. A critical safety procedure where the first arriving firefighter, usually the officer or incident commander, walks completely around the scene to get a full view of the area from all sides before committing crews to action.

"Can't see the exact pipe yet," he said. "But it's a big one. It's blowing through the dirt. Grab your shovels, but not the steel ones."

Why Not Steel? When you dig around flammable gas, even a small spark from metal-on-metal contact can set off an explosion. That's why we use special shovels made of fiberglass, copper, or other non-sparking materials. It doesn't guarantee safety, but it's one less reason to die.

The sharp, chemical stench of natural gas hit us before we even stepped out. It's artificial, sure, but once you know it, you never forget it. Like a rotten egg crawled into your sinuses and decided to set up camp.

What's That Smell? Natural gas is actually odorless. The distinct "rotten egg" smell comes from a chemical called mercaptan, which is added by gas companies as a safety measure. It's strong, foul, and impossible to ignore—which is exactly the point. If you smell it, it means there's a leak, and it's time to act quickly.

We masked up before moving in. My first breath fogged my mask for a second, then cleared. The guys and I checked each other's seals.

One nod. We moved in.

The scene was a mess from the construction work. Equipment and cones lay scattered near the burst pipe. The construction crew had already cleared out, and they were smart enough to back off the moment they heard the first warning sound. The excavator that hit the line sat idle nearby.

Now, that sound had grown. It was no longer a hiss, but a shriek. High-pitched. Relentless. The kind of noise that makes the hair on your neck stand up.

We started digging slowly and steadily around the underground pipe. Every few minutes, the dirt would collapse back in the hole, erasing whatever progress we'd made. Sweat poured down our backs. Our arms shook from the constant digging in our gear. Our knees sank deeper into the churned-up mud.

We rotated crews every 15–20 minutes to keep the momentum. Even with air tanks, you can feel the heat building inside your suit, baking your skin.

Second rotation, I was back in the hole. Mud to my shins. The ground getting softer. Darker.

Something wasn't right.

I took one step backward, and the ground gave out underneath me. I dropped straight down. Waist-deep in a pool of thick, brown sludge.

At first, I thought it was mud water.

Then it hit me.

I was surrounded by raw sewage!

I had fallen into a broken sewer line. Merde swirling around me. Up to my hips. Gas hissing above my head.

I tried to scramble out, but my boots slipped and squelched against the slick sides of the pit. I could hear the guys laughing through their masks. I didn't blame them. If I wasn't the one drowning in it, I would have laughed too. I probably looked like an armadillo rolling in a mud puddle.

Damn disgraceful.

I scrambled out and choked inside my mask. Every inch of my gear was drenched in filth. The stench clung to me like it had seeped into my skin.

Still, we kept working.

Not but a few minutes later, the city's other crews arrived to help us locate the line using a utility survey. That's when we realized that we weren't even close to the rupture. The main leak was deeper and off to the right.

So, we dug until the earth gave way, and we eventually found a fat gas main line, cleanly severed, spewing high-pressure gas like a storm drain in reverse.

The captain called for the Mustang clamp.

What's a Mustang Clamp? A Mustang clamp is a mechanical device designed to seal off a broken gas line under pressure. You slap it around the pipe, ratchet tighter and tighter, until you squeeze the leak shut, like clamping a hose.

We wrapped the pipe with the clamp. Cranked it down. One pump at a time. The gas flow slowed, then slowed again, until it finally stopped.

Finally.

We staggered back to the trucks, stripped off our filthy gear, and got our vitals checked. Lukewarm water from plastic bottles went down like gold. And waiting for us (thanks to the amazing canteen crew) was pizza.

Awesome people. Solid support.

It tasted like cardboard dipped in sewer water, but nobody cared.

We were alive.

We did the job.

Another day on the team.

Another day... *in the literal latrine.*

Chapter 14: One Step from Gone

Arson fires always seem to have a special kind of commotion to them.

Sometimes it's for insurance. Sometimes it's just because people like to watch things burn. I had never experienced anything like the scene of arson in the movies, where you're sprinting from fire to fire—until that one summer month.

We had fires nearly every shift. Sometimes, two or three fires a day. Units were tied up across the city, and streets were jammed with fire trucks and smoke hanging in the air like a ceiling.

It reminded me of the "white powder scares." I wasn't around for the real anthrax calls, but we experienced constant hoaxes. Still, they locked down buildings, tied up hazmat teams, and sent everyone into full protocol.

Anyway, back to the fire. See? This is what happens. I start reminiscing and forget I've got an actual story to tell.

When the tones dropped that night, it wasn't a medical call. It wasn't a fender-bender.

It was a fire!

"Residential structure fire." – dispatch said.

Now if you think your heart races on a medical call, you can't imagine the feeling when a real fire call drops. You bolt out of bed, sprinting half-dressed into the bay, and pull on gear as fast as humanly possible. You leap into the truck like it's a race car screaming off the starting line at Daytona.

Think of the movies *Backdraft* or *Ladder 49*. Fire eating the sky. Firefighters charging into hell. It's not far off—just without the soundtrack.

As we rolled out, I could already smell the burning plastic, drywall, and wood, all mixing together into one thick stench. At night, you don't see the billowing smoke from a distance like you would during the day. You smell it. You *feel* it in the air before you ever see it.

As we pulled down the block, the entire street was blacked out. The thick smoke choked every streetlamp and created a yellow haze. It was like we were creeping into another world.

We didn't even bother with the front door.

The captain had already called it—heavy fire showing from the Charlie side (the back of the house).

We'd make our push from the rear.

It was a small frame house, split into front and back sections. The layout was simple.

I jumped off the truck, grabbed the hose line, and waved for water. The driver charged it instantly. I bled the line, purged the air, and watched that first blast of water hit the door step like a firecracker.

We were ready.

When you're inside a fire, you stay low. Visibility is next to nothing. Thick smoke turns everything into shadows and shapes. You search with your hands, feel for walls, count your steps, and sweep your tools ahead like a blind man's cane. The smoke banks down. It's thick, black, ready to kill you.

Every breath you take is a battle that you don't even realize you're winning.

The captain and I pushed deep inside the home. Fire had already chewed through the ceiling, and the beams were exposed. The smoke was swirling like a living thing. We hit it hard, sweeping the water in a high-low pattern to break up the thermal layers. Windows were vented, plywood was torn away, and finally, enough smoke cleared for us to find the seat of the fire and to drown it. *Fast and clean.*

No victims. No secondary fire rooms. Just a building full of smoke and a street full of exhausted firefighters.

Then came Overhaul.

We started pulling the ceiling. Ripping up burnt furniture. Sifting through the wreckage to find hidden embers before they could reignite and torch the place again.

I stepped outside to grab a tool from the truck. The smoke had settled into a dense, low-hanging cloud that clung to everything. In the darkness, you could barely see your own hands, let alone anything beyond them.

The backyard was a mess. Paint on the old fence peeled from the heat and crumbled under my gloves as I brushed past the other firefighters. Yard lights struggled to cut through the haze, only making the darkness feel heavier.

I was moving aimlessly, just trying to find the damn New York hook. Then it happened.

I nearly walked straight into death.

One more step. Maybe two. And I would've landed square on a live power line. It was coiled through the wet, greasy backyard like a *viper* waiting to strike. A thick, tangled, black cable, which was perfectly hidden against the soot, mud, and standing water.

The captain grabbed my jacket and yanked me back hard. "Kid, watch where the fuck you're going! Live power line!" he barked.

Time froze.

Think of that scene in *The Hurt Locker*. Everything slows to a crawl, the noise fades, and every decision you've ever made flashes through your mind in perfect, terrifying clarity.

Now, obviously, the stakes were completely different. In my case, it was just me who could've been struck. In the movie, a single wrong move would blow up an entire city block. So yeah, not exactly the same, and I'm not trying to compare. But the feeling? The fear? That was real. I was scared straight.

My heart was pounding. Mouth dry. In that single second, everything could've ended. My career, maybe even my life, and all because I didn't look carefully enough. One missed detail, and that was all it would've taken.

Would it have killed me? Who knows. But I wasn't about to find out. I looked up at Captain Graves. He just shrugged, like it was nothing.

Just another day to him. Just another part of the job.

But for me, it was a reminder. A reminder that in this job, you don't get unlimited chances.

I've had close calls since then, but that night? That was the first time I realized just how *thin* the line really is between going home...
and not.

15. Rarely Done Right

I scored number three on the promotional exam, and in that moment, I was as proud of myself as I'd ever been. It wasn't just a promotion, it was validation. Months of grinding, studying, pushing myself forward.

I was now officially a Driver Engineer. Entrusted with one of the most impressive vehicles ever to roll down a public road: *the fire truck*. Let me tell you—there's nothing cooler.

I was pulling levers, cranking handles, dialing gauges, adjusting pressures, and making sure my crew got exactly what they needed at every fire. In the two years that I spent driving, I caught more fires than I can count. Each house fire, car fire, and commercial blaze was unique and unforgettable.

We once had a fire at a food processing plant that burned for over fourteen hours. Benny, Jay, and Louie were there, side by side, hammering the building with master streams from every angle. It was the kind of call where you're still on scene when the next crew shows up to relieve you. We worked all night, soaked in sweat and steam, just trying to beat it back.

My stories from behind that wheel could fill another book entirely. Every fire had its own personality, its own rhythm, its own challenges, and a moment that stayed with you long after the smoke cleared.

I drove under some tough captains. Although they were all different, and I of course preferred some more than others, I took something valuable from each one of them. The small stuff stuck. Like why the hose-bed nozzles were painted like traffic lights: *red on top, yellow in the middle, green at the bottom.*

Colors weren't just for looks. They had a purpose. Sure, the color coding made it easier to grab the right line when a captain barked out an order, especially in the dark or under pressure. But for us, everything had its own rhythm.

Red usually meant foam, and it was the line we pulled most often (*our go-to*). Yellow was versatile and a reliable middle-ground. Green was the grab-and-go line for quick hits.

It might sound simple, but during an active scene, especially at night, those colors mattered. You didn't have to fumble for labels or second-guess yourself. You just reached, pulled, and went.

Little things like that didn't just make you look sharp. They made the whole operation run smoother. But no amount of sharpness could save me from what happened next.

One of my last shifts at Center City Station went down in station lore.

As the Driver Engineer on the slowest truck in the house, I got stuck with the one assignment that I dreaded more than hose testing in August. Cooking. And you've got to understand something: I hate cooking. I miss the days when Hot Pockets were considered gourmet.

But at the firehouse? That would never fly. These guys acted like they were dining in a five-star restaurant. Everything had to be perfect. Multiple meals a day.

I had a few go-to meals, including some that my sister-in-law taught me, but my favorite was the Southwest Chipotle Wraps. The lunch dish that I lovingly called *The Chipotal.* Grilled chicken, lettuce, black beans, rice, corn, salsa, avocado, cheese, onions, tortillas, and a generous drizzle of Chipotle Ranch. Simple. Satisfying. Foolproof.

And yet, at Center City, they still found ways to complain. So I finally had enough.

One Sunday, officially known as "Fat Bastard Sunday" at the firehouse, things came to a head. Big breakfast. Hearty lunches. Sports games. Dessert. Basically, we ate like absolute animals.

That day, they wanted chicken wings. I grilled those wings with genuine effort. All the guys gathered to eat, including my buddy "D." He is a solid firefighter, outstanding medic, and one of the nicest guys that I know, and he had been on rescue calls all morning. Running nonstop with no breaks.

When he finally sat down to eat, he took one bite and erupted.

"Erik, these wings are raw!"

He… was… pissed. And honestly, he had every right to be. The last thing you want after back-to-back rescue calls is chicken sushi. Reluctantly, I threw the wings back on the grill and cooked them properly.

D didn't get sick. Turns out not every undercooked wing gives you salmonella (statistically, it's about 1 in 25,000 chickens). But the damage was done. Morale had tanked, and the insults flew. A few guys even threatened to order pizza in protest.

And that's when I decided:

Revenge was on the menu! *(index finger raised dramatically, like a wise and slightly petty narrator.)*

***

Dinner rolled around, and I asked the probie (just under a year on the job) to take everyone's steak orders. He was eager to please, and he walked around with pen and paper, carefully jotting down how each firefighter wanted their steak cooked.

When he handed me that neatly prepared list, I looked him dead in the eye… and tore it clean in half.

His jaw dropped.

"Watch and learn," I told him, tossing the paper in the trash.

Then… I grilled every single steak—the exact same way.

Rare.

Bloody, flavorful, and unapologetic. That night, out of pure spite, the guys ate their steaks my way. No exceptions. Not even the captain.

When I dropped the platter on the kitchen counter, I said, "Dinner is served, boys. Hope you like 'em rare."

They stared in disbelief. Then the knives came out. Literally. One by one, they cut into their steaks, and blood pooled across their plates.

"These steaks are still alive!" someone shouted.

"Perfect," I said, calmly slicing into mine and savoring every bite.

They were furious. Half the crew stormed back outside to re-cook their steaks. Honestly, I couldn't blame them. But I wasn't sorry either. I knew exactly what I was doing, and I enjoyed every second of it.

But… karma has a funny way of catching up.

Just a few shifts later, it would be my last shift at Center City, at least on the Heavy Rescue truck. Ironically, getting moved off the slowest truck meant no more kitchen duty. And in a way, I got the last laugh.

Life as a Driver Engineer was never dull. But after a couple of years, it was time to take the next step.

Chapter 16: Walk Away

Just two years after becoming a Driver Engineer, I hit the biggest milestone of my career. I was officially promoted to Lieutenant. It felt surreal stepping into a role for which I had always yearned. The Lieutenant is the one who leads from the front, remains calm in the chaos, and earns trust when everything's on the line.

But don't get it twisted, I wasn't suddenly some cocky hard-ass or badge-flipper writing up the guys. That's not my style. You'd have to be a real piece of work to get disciplined by me. What I expect is simple:

Do your job respectfully.

Know your addresses. Time is everything in this job, and you cannot afford to get lost.

Know your protocols.

Start an IV with your eyes closed, and worst-case scenario, be ready to surgically cut someone's throat to save them. *That's it.* I don't care if you make pot coffee or clean the bathrooms on time. Just be ready when the tones drop.

I'd like to think I'm the kind of lieutenant who guys want to work with, and not because I'm soft, but because I back them when it counts.

Reed and AJ were on the first team that I led as an LT. I was now in control of a Rescue (ambulance) and a crew of two very solid guys. Reed was a full-time boat captain when he wasn't in bunker gear. The man could navigate 40-foot fishing charters like he was born on the water. AJ was an EMT instructor on his off days. When he wasn't running calls, I'd catch him grading tests between runs. He's one of the smartest guys I know, and one of my best friends to this day.

We were stationed in the "Wild, Wild West"—the city's west side. Shootings. Stabbings. House fires. Overdoses. That district didn't hold back. Sure, 9-11 got abused like it did everywhere else, but when the tones dropped out there, the calls were consistently more serious than those in most other districts. It wasn't a matter of *if* something wild was going down, it was just a matter of *when*.

That shift started like any other. A few calls, including some overdoses and some chest pains. Nothing out of the ordinary. We were handling it, and I was proud of my guys. We even managed to get some rest that night.

Until 6:45 a.m.

The tones dropped.

"Overturned vehicle with entrapment."

108

My eyes popped open. I was on my feet, strapping on my radio and pulling on my boots, before my brain was even fully awake. I keyed up the radio, "Rescue 1 en route." Then switched over to Tac 1.

Tac Channels (short for tactical channels) are designated radio frequencies used by first responders to communicate directly with one another on active scenes, separate from main dispatch, so as to not tie up the radio and to allow for more effective communication.

I threw open the bay door, jumped into the front passenger seat of the rescue (the "box"), and pulled the CAD toward me. The call details hit like a gut punch: multiple vehicles. Multiple people trapped. Rollover. It was going to be a big one.

What's CAD? Computer-Aided Dispatch is basically the digital nerve center of 9-1-1. When someone calls for help, the dispatcher enters the info into the system, and CAD pushes it out to our rigs in real-time. It gives us the address, the call's description, notes from the caller, and any extra details, like gate codes or "beware of dog" warnings. It updates live, so if the caller adds something like "patient just passed out," we should see it before we even pull up.

AJ hopped in the driver seat, Reed in the back, and just like that, we were off. We headed down one of the busiest roads in the city, already stacked with morning commuters.

As we approached the intersection, we had the green light. Across from us, a line of box trucks formed in the turn lane, and they all were waiting to make a left—their left, our right. They completely blocked our view of oncoming traffic. We slowed to be sure. Looked left. Looked right. Everything seemed clear. It looked clear.

But it wasn't.

From behind one of those box trucks, a red SUV shot out, recklessly swerved hard into the intersection, and drilled us at a very high speed.

T-boned.

Full force.

Our rig jolted like we'd hit a landmine. I don't even remember what I yelled. I just grabbed the dash and braced for impact as we were shoved forward.

Time slowed.

I saw spots. Felt dazed. Like someone rang my bell hard but didn't knock me out. AJ was trying to regain control of the rig when we rolled to a stop just before the light pole. I turned back to find Reed down on the floor.

"Is everyone okay?!" I shouted.

"I'm good," AJ said. Reed grunted. "Yeah… I think so."

"Geez! We just got hit," I said, still trying to make sense of it.

I grabbed the mic.

"Rescue 1 to dispatch—**we've been struck by another vehicle.** We need another rescue to respond to the original call. We are out of service."

Just like that, the call we were racing toward was someone else's job. *We had our own emergency now.*

I tried to open my door, but it was jammed. The back doors were crushed, so we all had to climb out through the front driver's side. One by one, squeezing past broken glass and twisted metal.

When we finally stepped out, we looked like a bunch of dazed drunk guys staggering out of a dive bar at 3 a.m. Stumbling. Disoriented. Still buzzing from the adrenaline.

That's when I spotted one of our off-duty lieutenants, Bert. He had been on his way to work, but happened to be right there at the intersection when it all went down. He was already out of his car, talking to the driver who hit us.

The small red SUV was mangled from its front bumper all the way through its cab. The driver's legs were partially pinned, but he was conscious and alert. Bert looked over, locked eyes with me, and with just a few calm words, helped snap me out of the fog.

I took one look at that guy and knew it was at least a level 2 trauma.

Level 2 Trauma. *Refers to a patient with serious injuries that doesn't meet the highest level of trauma criteria (Level 1), but still requires rapid intervention and specialized care.*

Another rescue already had rolled up (one of the crews originally assigned to the accident on our original call). They diverted to help us. Without missing a beat, we all got to work. No time to waste.

We got a cervical collar on the driver of the SUV right away and secured his neck. The crews grabbed the backboard while Bert worked the door. It was bent and jammed, but not beyond our muscle. We didn't need fancy tools, just grit and coordination. After some pressure and pulling, the door popped free.

With hands on, we guided the guy out gently. His legs were sore, but not broken. Still conscious. Still breathing. We slid him onto the backboard and transferred him to the stretcher that was already staged and ready. He was alive, alert, and breathing on his own.

It hit me hard. He was okay. *We* were okay. But I couldn't shake the guilt. We were supposed to be at that first call. We were supposed to be helping those people. But this job has a way of teaching you lessons. You can't be everywhere at once, and sometimes bad things happen. And sometimes, *surviving is the biggest win.*

Turns out, the guy who hit us didn't even have a license and was driving recklessly. As for our rig? Totaled.

Thankfully, the original accident, the one we were racing to, had been handled. The patients were successfully extricated and, from what we heard, in good health.

***

It was closer to 11 a.m. before we got back to the station. Forget about going home at 8 a.m. shift change.

But Reed still got to go home to his girl and the fishing charter. AJ made it back to his wife and kids. And I got to walk through the door, hug my wife, and hold my dog—grateful for the life we had, and for the son we were about to meet.

That... was a good day.

And in this line of work... sometimes, that's all you can ask for.

Chapter 17: The Miracle of Ms. Rachel

Fast-forward a few years, and I'm training the next hiring classes on the rescue truck. We get a lot of students that ride at the firehouse—EMTs, paramedics, and even the occasional med-school intern trying to figure out what the hell we do out here. And to be fair, most of them don't really get it until they see it.

We're not just a fire department, we're a rescue department too. That means at one moment, you could be crawling into a burning building, and the next, you are cracking someone's chest open on their front lawn. That's just the way it is. Dual-certified. Cross-trained. All hazards.

As a preceptor, I get a front-row seat to the future of the profession. By the time these kids get to their final semester, they've already survived the gauntlet, including EMT school, paramedic school, clinicals, and fire school. They've got the books memorized and the patches to prove it; but, the truth is that just because you've read the books, does not mean that you can do the job.

That's where we come in.

Jordan was one of those students. Big dude and built like a linebacker. Quiet as a church mouse. Not in a dumb way. He was just observant. Humble. And that alone made him stand out.

He didn't butt into firehouse talk. Didn't try to teach guys who've been here 20 years how to do their job. He just kept his head down, asked the right questions at the right time, and was hungry to learn.

Even with that, he was still green. He missed a couple of basic things early on, like taking a blood pressure reading or listening to lung sounds. But he owned it. He didn't make excuses. And I respect the hell out of that.

I told him straight, "I don't care if you mess up. I care if you lie about it. Stay honest, stay open, and I'll teach you everything I know."

***

It was a busy shift with back-to-back calls, station training, and a trip to the fleet shop because our truck decided to light up like a Christmas tree with warning lights. At our station, there were two rescues running nonstop, and Jordan was bouncing between both units. Double the calls. Double the chaos.

Just after lunchtime, I could see the kid was wiped, and we still hadn't eaten. Another call dropped, and I told him, "Hey man, go ahead. Grab lunch with the other crew. We'll handle this next one."

Jordan shook his head. "Sir, with all due respect, I'd rather ride with you guys."

I grinned. "Can't blame you. We are the best crew in the department."

Without missing a beat, one of the guys from the other rescue shot back, "Yeah, if the competition was for most snacks eaten during a shift."

He wasn't wrong. I'm a damn snack machine. Skittles, Twix, KitKats. Mostly candy. If it fits in my pocket, it's fair game. Fruit? Love it too. Bananas, apples, oranges. You name it, and I've got it rolling around the cab somewhere.

But my true weakness? Chips.

Have you ever had those *Terra* chips? The ones that come in the sleek black bag that practically screams, "I look healthier than I am"? Inside, it's a crunchy kaleidoscope of root veggies, sweet potatoes, parsnips, taro, and yucca, and they're all sliced thin and kettle-cooked until they're crispy enough to chip a tooth.

Each chip looks like it came from a different planet: purple, orange, gold, and even that weird white with purple veins like it's got a backstory. They've got this earthy, salty-sweet thing going on—like potato chips went to a yoga retreat and came back enlightened. And yeah, I eat them like I'm doing something good for my body... while demolishing the whole bag by myself in ten minutes flat.

As I write this, I'm 16 hours into a 36-hour fast—my first one. My beautiful wife, Katie, somehow convinced me into this madness. Am I slipping? Am I about to cave and grab a bag of chips? I'm starting to feel like Newman in that *Seinfeld* episode, where he is staring at Kramer and seeing a giant, roasted turkey. Ahhh… I'm losing it.

Anyway, I digress.

The day rolled on, and the calls kept coming, including an allergic reaction and a hypoglycemic patient. Then came another. A woman on fat burners. Her heart was racing, and her blood pressure had dropped well below the normal limits. Jordan grabbed the IV kit, and he was ready to throw in a line like most eager students.

It's a common instinct. Every student wants to jump straight into advanced life support to push meds and to use what they learned in class.

But what they don't realize is that basic life support saves lives just as often—*sometimes more.*

BLS Vs ALS. *BLS, or Basic Life Support, is the term for the basics: CPR, slapping on an AED, giving oxygen, and stopping bleeding. It's the kind of care you can provide without needles. ALS, or Advanced Life Support, comes into play when the real tools are needed: IV's, advanced meds, intubation, all the fancy stuff we use when things start going south fast. Basically, BLS keeps the engine running, ALS pops the hood and fixes what's broken when the engine is really sputtering.*

"Hold up," I told him. "Before you start that IV, lift her legs and put her in a modified Trendelenburg."

I gave him the quick rundown, like we always do.

"BLS before ALS."

"Every time you move a patient, reassess, and that's your shot to catch what others miss."

I didn't come up with this stuff. These are just lessons passed down from mentors and salty vets who knew their stuff.

Modified Trendelenburg. A classic BLS move. You elevate the legs, keeping the head flat or slightly tilted. It helps return blood to the vital organs. It's not flashy, but it works fast and often buys time when nothing else will.

Jordan nodded, adjusted the stretcher, and got to work in the back of the moving rescue. Lights and sirens. Real time, real pressure.

That's how we train. You can't learn this job in a classroom. You need to feel the bumps in the road while you're threading an IV. You need to hear the radio chatter and the screaming siren while you're making clinical decisions. That's the only way to build the muscle memory that'll save someone when everything goes sideways.

We don't wait for perfect conditions. We practice during the calls that aren't life-or-death, so that when we get the ones that are, we're sharp, proficient, and ready.

Now to be clear, I don't ask my guys to do anything that I wouldn't do myself. Hell, sometimes I jump in and start a line too—just to keep myself honest. This job doesn't care how long you've been with the Department. You've got to earn your stripes every shift.

Jordan fumbled with the IV a bit, which is normal, but he kept his composure. We talked him through the steps. *Find the bounce. Wait for the pop. Don't squeeze the plastic. Occlude ahead of the catheter.*

Line secure. Saline locked.

He looked up like he'd just hit the game-winner.

And here's the part that I love. By the time he finished the IV, her blood pressure already began to climb. Her heart rate started to settle. We didn't even have to push fluids. That leg elevation alone started to stabilize her.

Just like that, we rolled into the ER with normal vital signs. That's the goal. Bring 'em in better than you found 'em. Basic or advanced. If it saves a life, it's gold.

***

Dinner rolled around, and just after 7 p.m., the tones dropped. Another call.

"Pediatric allergic reaction."

"Jordan," I told him, "go grab some food and head home. It's been a long day."

He looked at me and said, "If it's alright with you, sir, I'd rather ride one more with you guys."

And you already know how that went.

Now, I've been doing this long enough to know how fast allergic reactions can go downhill. Adult cases are fairly simple. You hit 'em with some Benadryl, maybe a small dose of epinephrine, and most of the time, they bounce back.

But babies?

Babies can hold on for a while, and then they crash like a wave out of nowhere. Once their airway goes, the fight to bring them back gets a whole lot harder.

I grabbed the CAD as it lit up, scrolling through the notes while we rolled.

"Six-month-old," I called out. "Flushed skin, difficulty breathing. Mom pulled over in the street—sounds bad boys so be ready."

I glanced back at Jordan. "Hang tight on this one. If it goes south, we need space to work."

These calls aren't the time for hands-on training. Sometimes, the best way to learn is just to watch and to take it all in.

We arrived to find a young mom holding her baby on the median of a busy road, with an off-duty cop standing by her, shielding them from traffic. The mom was panicked, her eyes wide, and she was clutching that baby like her life depended on it.

I locked eyes with the baby, and my stomach twisted. Fully flushed. Labored breathing. Hives spreading across his chest and face.

He was compensating, but he could crash at any moment.

We loaded them both onto the stretcher (mom and baby together). My crew, Mikey and Joey, snapped into action. No hesitation. Everything was textbook

Epinephrine 1:1000.

Benadryl.

Solu-Medrol.

Three different medications. Three different injection sites.

Mikey took the lead. And man, you could tell how careful he was. He knelt down, speaking softly to the mom while cradling that baby's little leg. His hands were steady. Each poke was deliberate, gentle, and controlled.

The baby cried hard, but he cried. And in our world, that's what matters. That means the airway is still open. That means that we've got time.

We kept blow-by oxygen flowing, and I watched that baby's chest rise. Each breath was a little deeper than the last. The redness started to fade. His oxygen levels climbed. His heart rate dropped to something far less scary.

We were turning the corner.

Jordan stood back and watched it all. Absorbed every detail. He understood that this wasn't a training moment—*it was a save.*

***

As we arrived at the hospital, the baby was stable, and the mom was clutching his tiny hand with tears in her eyes. I slid back into the lieutenant's seat and started filling out the report. Just routine work now. Document the vitals, meds, and timeline. The crisis had passed, and the paperwork had begun.

Then I heard it. Soft, familiar music playing from the mother's phone.

🎵 "Can you say mama, mama, can you say mama's name?" 🎵

I leaned over the stretcher and smiled. "Is that… Ms. Rachel?"

She laughed. "Yeah, we just started showing it to him. It seems to calm him down."

And man, that hit me right in the chest. My son's favorite show.

I don't know what it is about that woman's voice, but it's magic. I sat there for a second, watching that baby breathe and hearing that song in the background, *and it was like I was home again.* My wife. My kid. Dinner on the stove. It all hit me at once.

That's what this job does to you. One moment, you're saving a life. The next, you're seeing your own in someone else's.

The boys nudged me. "That one's gonna stay with you, huh?"

I nodded with my eyes still on the baby. "Yeah... baby calls always do. Hits different these days though, with my own at home."

We treated that kid like he was ours. Because when you do this job right, every patient becomes family, even if it's just for ten minutes.

Jordan walked away from that shift with a little more fire in his eyes.

And me?

I walked away knowing this was still the **best job in the world.**

Chapter 18: From Above

It was just another shift on the north side.

We'd been posted at one of the slower stations in town, where the calls were usually mild, like lift assists, nosebleeds, and the occasional diabetic check. So when the tones dropped for a "sick person," it barely raised an eyebrow. That call is one of the most common dispatches that we get. Vague. Harmless-sounding.

I had Joey riding up front and JJ in the back. Solid crew. Trustworthy. The address we were going to wasn't far, and the home was in one of the nicer parts of town. We pulled up to a well-kept house with perfect hedges and a welcome mat that looked brand-new.

A woman answered the door, calm but concerned.

"My husband's just… he's not feeling right."

He was sitting on the edge of the bed, and he was pale with his shoulders slumped slightly forward. Not diaphoretic. Not gasping. But off.

Maybe it's cardiac. Maybe it's the flu. Maybe it's just nothing. But something in his posture, his skin, the way his eyes tracked us— something told me this wasn't going to be routine.

I turned back to my guys. "Let's get him on the monitor and see what we're working with."

JJ grabbed the blood pressure cuff. Joey hooked up the leads. Meanwhile, I talked to the wife and pulled history, which included prior cardiac issues, meds, recent illnesses, and allergies. That's the real art of EMS: one team collecting numbers and the other collecting context.

The 12-lead came back. There was some ST elevation. Subtle, but it was there. Some reciprocal depression in the inferior leads.

ST elevation is a finding on a 12-lead EKG, a tool we use to look at the heart's electrical activity. It shows up as a little "bump" on the monitor, but that bump can mean something big. When we see ST elevation, it often means part of the heart muscle isn't getting blood, and it is a possible sign of a heart attack in progress. It's like the heart is raising a red flag.

Now, I could write two more books trying to explain how to interpret a 12-lead EKG. It's a language of its own. But for now, just take my word that this wasn't normal.

"Sir," I said, kneeling beside the bed, "there's something a little off in the picture of your heart. We can't say exactly what from here, but I'd like to take you to the hospital to have a cardiologist take a closer look."

He nodded. "Yeah, of course. Whatever you think."

I stood up and turned to speak with the patient's wife. That's when Joey's voice cut through the room—**"LT…"**

I turned back just in time to see the man, just sitting upright, suddenly collapse backward into the mattress, like someone had flipped a switch and shut him off.

Joey was already at his side, fingers to the neck.

"LT… I've got no pulse."

One look was all it took. That stare. Wide-eyed. Vacant. Lifeless. The unmistakable dead stare you never forget.

The monitor showed a shockable rhythm, but we didn't have the pads on yet. You don't just throw defibrillator pads on anyone without cause. It has to be warranted, confirmed, and done with purpose.

"Get him on the floor!" I barked.

We moved fast, but with control. In sync, we lowered him gently and laid him flat on the carpet. Joey jumped on compressions without hesitation. JJ already was prepping the IV line. I grabbed the combo pads, setting them up for immediate defibrillation. If the rhythm held, we weren't wasting a second.

About twenty seconds passed with just high-quality CPR. No meds. No shocks. Just hands on the chest, fighting to buy him time.

And then—**he gasped.**

He took a ragged, desperate pull of air, like something had yanked him back from the edge. It felt as if life itself had been injected straight into his lungs.

Like God Himself whispered… *Not yet.*

His eyes fluttered open. Confused. Alive.

"What… what happened?"

"We believe you went into cardiac arrest from a heart attack," I told him gently. "But you're back. You're with us now."

His eyes welled up. He didn't say much. He just nodded, like he understood everything and nothing at once. Moments like that don't need a lot of words. The look on his face said enough.

We loaded him onto the stretcher and started moving. Protocols kicked in—notifications to the ER, observations of the monitor, stabilization of the vitals. Everything we train for, everything we hope for, playing out exactly as it should.

A textbook cardiac arrest save, if such a thing even exists.

But this chapter isn't just about the save.

Haven't you ever wondered what happens when you die? I mean, have you really wondered what it's like to cross over, even for a moment? Or do you actually cross all the way over if God isn't ready for you? Have you ever wanted to ask someone who's actually been there and back?

JJ, quiet and somewhat spiritual, leaned over as we approached the hospital. He'd been thinking, like he always does after calls like this. Reflecting. Processing. Doing the kind of soul-work that most of us bury under protocol and sarcasm.

He looked at the man and asked, "Sir... if you don't mind me asking, when you were unconscious... did you see anything? Anything at all?"

The man looked right at JJ. No hesitation.

"I saw you guys," he said. "From above."

That got our attention.

"I was watching all of you from up there—above the bed looking down," he said, slowly lifting a hand to point at me. "I saw *you*, kneeling at my side... *him*, doing chest compressions... and *you*, over there, doing something with a needle," which we figured meant starting an IV.

He paused, his voice softer now.

"And then, just like that, I felt this rush of air, like someone pushed life back into me. That's when I knew... it wasn't my time. Not yet."

We didn't say much after that. Didn't have to.

We all glanced at each other, goosebumps on our arms, and the truck's cabin was thick with something more than adrenaline.

I'm not here to tell you what to believe. I've worked with atheists, skeptics, Christians, Jews, Buddhists, and people who worship the New York Jets. But I'll tell you this: moments like that change people.

For me?

I know there's something (or Someone) greater out there. Call it God, fate, the universe—whatever fits your belief. But moments like that? They don't feel like coincidence. We're too intricate, too fragile, too full of purpose to be explained away as random biology.

That man got a second chance.

And maybe, just maybe, we got a reminder... that sometimes, Someone *is* looking out for us.

From above.

Chapter 19: Mangled Motorcycle

From as far back as I can remember, motorcycles have been an interest of mine. Same for a lot of guys that I know. The sense of unreal speed, something untamed, like a Cheetah tearing through the desert.

It called to you.

When I was 15 or 16, my first car was a Pontiac G6. Now, at that age, I thought that I was hot stuff. "So fly like a G6, fly like a G6," just like the song said. Except the G6 wasn't a private jet. It wasn't even close. It was a hooptie, barely limping along, and I wasn't beating anybody in any race.

Still, the idea of speed stayed with me. Until reality checked me.

Both of my older brothers were in separate motorcycle accidents. One had to be airlifted from the scene. Thank God he and his passenger survived, but that moment hit me hard at a young age.

In an instant, I realized how thin the line is between life and death on a crotch rocket. What is survivable in a car could be fatal on a bike. That truth never left me. Not when I became a firefighter. And definitely not when I started responding to motorcycle accidents myself.

***

Midday.

Call drops.

"Motorcycle accident."

My regular crew and I already happened to be out on the road. AJ driving. "What are we looking at, LT?" he asked, glancing over at me.

I scanned the CAD screen. "Vehicle versus motorcycle," I said flatly, code for, *this probably isn't going to end well.*

But no matter how many times you've heard it, nothing ever really prepares you for the real thing. Within seconds, we were on scene.

A crumpled car.

A shattered motorcycle.

And a man lying still.

But he wasn't just down—he was **entangled.** As I got closer, I could see that the bike had wrapped around him like it was a part of his body. Plastic shattered everywhere. Steel piercing into his limbs.

His arms and legs were twisted in ways that human bones aren't supposed to move.

Something that should've been unsurvivable.

And somehow—*he was awake.*

Shock can do crazy things. He was staring up, dazed but breathing.

Holding on.

I knelt beside him. "We're here, brother. You're not alone. We've got your back. We're gonna take good care of you."

We didn't waste a second.

AJ led the dismantling with absolute focus. I had my best guys on it.

Piece by piece, we untangled him. Pulling away fragments of plastic and metal. Careful not to move what didn't need moving, but quick enough to beat the clock. The **Golden Hour** was ticking.

I alerted the ER. "Trauma alert. Male patient, early twenties. Multiple deformities. Conscious but deteriorating. ETA 10 minutes."

The backup engine crew arrived and dropped a backboard. We slid the young man onto it like he was made of glass.

Everything moved very quickly after that. We loaded him into the rescue, and the doors slammed shut behind us. The engine firefighter jumped into the cab and punched the gas.

In the back, we locked in. He was starting to fade, drifting in and out. His breathing was shallow, but still present. We secured his airway, got an IV established, and placed the monitor pads on his chest.

As I've said before, you don't throw pads on just anybody. *AED* pads are placed preemptively only if you think a patient might go into cardiac arrest at any moment.

In this case, it wasn't a matter of if—it was when.

But somehow...

He held on.

We hit the trauma bay like a hurricane. We sprinted through the ER doors, and doctors and nurses fell into step beside us.

We offloaded him with a pulse. Still breathing.

And still... in the fight.

We did our job.

***

Weeks had passed. Months, maybe even a year. Honestly, I had moved onto hundreds of other calls since that day.

Until one afternoon, I ran into a buddy. Said he knew someone who had been in a bad motorcycle crash, and it was bad enough that they thought he'd never walk again.

"That was your call," he said. "You guys kept him alive. He's walking now."

I froze. The memory of his face came rushing back.

My heart slammed into my chest. I just sat there, and I felt something I don't let myself feel too often. *Pride.*

"Thanks, brother," I said quietly. "That means more than you know."

And it did.

Because this job isn't about the glory. It's about moments like that. Moments you don't even know that you earned until life throws them back at you like a gift.

Held together by hope, by hustle, and by hands that refused to give up.

Chapter 20: Walk-Up from the South

Seven years into the position, I've learned that being a lieutenant means standing in the space between the chaos of the calls and the rhythm of the firehouse. It's a role that requires balance. You are part leader, part teammate, and constantly navigating both the culture and the job itself.

Now, around the firehouse, being a lieutenant carries a strange tone. For many, it means you're back on the rescue, but not riding the engine (where most firefighters prefer to be). The rescue is where the nasty stuff happens. Blood, vomit, overdoses, psych calls, nursing homes, and those long transports.

These are the calls that test your patience, your stomach, and sometimes, your compassion.

It's easy to see why some avoid it. But over time, I've come to see the rescue for what it really is—up close and unfiltered *humanity*. It's raw. It's real. And it's where I've learned the most, not only about this job, but also about the people.

And... about myself.

It's easy to fall into the mindset that you're stuck, especially when you see others climbing ranks or riding trucks that don't reek of Clorox and regret.

But honestly? It's all about *perspective*.

I've always respected those who chose to stay on the rescue for 15, 18, even 20+ years. The ones who kept showing up, shift after shift, without losing their sense of purpose. No bitterness. No burnout. Just *steady,* solid work. Because let's be real, starting your shift angry at the world doesn't help anyone, and it sure as hell doesn't help your patients.

I've come to love the rescue truck and the freedom that comes with it. You're still an officer and still leading your crew—holding the standard, staying sharp, and stepping in when it counts. But rescue gives you a different kind of rhythm. More autonomy. More critical medical calls. More face-to-face moments where it's just you, the patient, and the clock.

Don't get me wrong. The engine will always be the heartbeat of the fire service. It's where most of us begin. Attacking fires, stretching lines, and making the grab. That is the foundation. Truck work is just as vital. Venting, searching, and throwing ladders. It all matters.

We may not always be the ones stretching the first line, but we're still there when it counts. You can still be part of the search. Still pull someone out. Still be shoulder to shoulder when things go sideways.

But rescue isn't a step down. It's not a step up either. **It's just a different seat in the same fight.**

One team.

One mission.

Because when a life's on the line, it's all hands on deck, showing up and getting it done together.

***

That night felt like so many others before it. The city buzzed with tension, and you could feel it in your bones. The kind of shift where the tones drop the second you step into the shower or finally close your eyes.

We were staging for scene safety on the south side of the incident, just outside where PD was working, but close enough to feel the ripple. The dispatcher's voice was tight and clipped. The CAD chirped nonstop with fresh updates. Multiple shootings. Possible drive-by.

Something big was bubbling over, and it wasn't even midnight.

We were parked about a mile away from the incident, windows down, and we were just waiting for the all-clear. I leaned out the passenger window, one arm on the door, listening to the radio chatter and trying to piece things together.

The hum of the city never really stops. In the distance, I could hear the low metallic groan of the train heading our way. You could feel the subtle vibration in our truck. The horns weren't blasting; it was just a low, drawn-out moan. Almost like the city itself was sighing under the weight of whatever was coming.

That train always ran in our city, and in our world, it could be either your saving grace or the reason someone dies waiting.

It had just started rolling behind us when the situation changed.

That's when I saw him.

A male, late twenties, walking right in front of our truck. Blood running down his face and soaking through his shirt.

My first reaction was all instinct. I yanked my arm in and rolled the window up fast. Looked at AJ. He looked at me. Eyes wide. Heart pounding. It's crazy how fast your brain jumps to the worst-case scenario when you're not ready for it.

But within seconds, everything shifted.

He was hurt.

The guy had come stumbling up from the south side of the street, bleeding, dazed, and locking eyes with us like we were his last shot.

I keyed up the mic. "Dispatch, Rescue 1. I have a possible GSW victim that just walked up to our unit. We're still at staging. Request PD code 3 to our location."

Out here, you don't assume anything. Just because someone's bleeding, doesn't mean they're not a threat. I stepped out cautiously, but quickly. His eyes were half-closed, but his face said it all. Pain. Panic. Desperation.

"I need help. I've been shot," he said, barely getting the words out.

We moved fast and got him into the truck.

"You carrying anything?" I asked.

"No. Nothing. I swear."

I've learned to always ask, because even while helping a patient, a hidden weapon or knife could accidentally discharge or cause harm. It's happened before.

First priority: strip him down. Check for entry and exit wounds.

One gunshot to the face with no exit wound. Another to the chest with an exit out the back. We sealed both torso wounds with occlusive dressings. Wrapped his head tight. The bleeding hadn't stopped, but it was slow. Controlled.

I keyed up the mic again: "Dispatch, notify the ER. We've got one adult male trauma alert, approximately 24 year old, GSW to the face and chest, GCS 15. Paramedic Mendoza. ETA ten minutes."

The clock had started. The **Golden Hour** was underway.

I looked at the crew.

"Everything else, we do en route. Let's move."

***

Within five minutes, we were rolling. Lights on. Sirens screaming. And somehow, it still felt quiet inside the cab. That kind of quiet that makes the outside noise seem distant and dull.

In the back, the patient was awake. He was breathing and speaking softly.

He told us that he was shot in a drive-by just north of our location. Somehow, he ran south through yards and in between houses, bleeding the entire way. He said he saw our flashing lights through the trees and followed them like a *beacon* from a lighthouse.

We had parked west of the train tracks on purpose. The train was already rolling by when the patient walked up on us. If we had staged on the east side and waited for PD to clear us in, we would've been trapped. The patient might never have seen us or been able to reach us, and we would've been forced to delay transport. Watching that train crawl by while ten critical minutes slipped away would have been catastrophic.

Could've cost him his life.

PD met us on the road and gave us an escort. Their lights and sirens blazed as they cleared intersections like a wave splitting the sea. It's wild how fast they move, but that chaos creates just enough order for us to do our job.

We hit the hospital bay hot, dropped the stretcher, and rolled him straight through the trauma doors.

"You're in good hands, my man. Best hospital in the state," I told him.

He glanced up—barely. Just a half nod, blood crusting on his face and eyes fading.

Another call in the books. Another stretcher soaked. Another rescue left in pieces. Gloves tossed, wrappers on the floor, and gear scattered like the aftermath of a fight.

Because that's exactly what it was.

***

The cops came in a few minutes later, shaking their heads. "How the hell did he walk up on you guys?"

Same question we were asking ourselves. *Were we staged too close? What if someone had followed him? What if a second drive-by had rolled through while he was at our truck?*

And then there was the train, always the damn train. *Should we have staged on the other side? Waited longer for the scene to clear?*

It's a gamble every time.

Split-second decisions with no rewind button. That night, it went our way. Because sometimes, the call doesn't come through dispatch.

Sometimes, it walks right up to your truck. Bleeding, scared, and praying you are still out there and willing to help.

Chapter 21: Controlled Chaos

It was a typical evening at the "Wild, Wild West."

Now, traditionally, Murphy's Law means: *"Anything that can go wrong, will go wrong."* And in our business, that saying holds up more times than I care to count. But I've always liked the version from the movie *Interstellar* a little better:

"Murphy's Law doesn't mean something bad will happen. It means that whatever can happen, will happen."

And on days like that, both versions applied. Because when you're the only rescue available and the city lights up, *everything* that can happen usually *does happen.*

Then came the tones:

"Vehicle accident. Car on fire."

Before dispatch could even finish the sentence, I was already out of my chair, yelling into the hallway, "Let's move, boys!"

I ran straight for my gear. Bunker pants, jacket, and boots. That part comes without thinking. It's pure muscle memory. In our line of work, if there's even a *chance* someone's trapped inside a burning vehicle, you don't wait. You move. You prepare for the worst and hope to God you're wrong. I've heard the stories of crews that went in and made those last-second rescues out of burning vehicles. Sometimes, you get them out. Sometimes, you don't. But either way, *you go in ready.*

As we pulled out of the station and turned onto the street, Mikey spotted a thick, black column of smoke rising in the distance. It was already towering over the horizon.

We didn't need directions.

That was our scene.

I turned to Joey in the jump seat and locked eyes with him. "If there's someone in that car, we don't hesitate. We go in, get them, and get out if they're viable."

We turned the corner and saw it. One car, fully engulfed in flames. Fire roared twenty feet into the air, lighting up the night like a scene from a war zone. It was bright. Violent. Unreal.

All I could see was the car burning like a furnace. The heat was intense. Flames danced across the hood and roof. Tires popped like gunfire. The smoke was thick, chemical, and choking. My eyes moved fast from the passenger seat of my truck, scanning for victims and desperate to find someone *before* it was too late.

Meanwhile, dispatch was still rattling off call notes like we were miles away. I grabbed the radio and cut her off mid-sentence.

"Rescue 1 to dispatch—stand by. We're on scene with one vehicle fire, fully involved. Start me a second rescue and show me assuming command. I'll advise further."

I snapped to Mikey, "Bunk out and meet me at the car!"

"Lt, we've got a trauma," he shouted, pointing to a man lying motionless on the median to our right, about fifty feet from the car fire

And just like that, my focus shifted. What started as a car fire with a possible rescue turned into something bigger. In that instant, I went from preparing to pull someone out of a burning vehicle to realizing we had multiple critical patients.

They teach us not to let it happen. In the fire academy, in medic school, it's drilled into you: *don't let your world shrink.* But in moments like this? It shrinks on its own.

Your job is to fight it back.

Control the chaos.

Control your mind.

I keyed up the mic again. "Dispatch, we've got one victim down in the roadway. Unknown if breathing. Start me a third rescue."

Mikey then dropped to the man sprawled in the intersection. "LT—he's pulseless!"

"Start compressions," I said without hesitation, my tone leaving no room for doubt.

He was critical. Severe trauma, no breathing, and no pulse. There was no time to wait and even less room for error.

My job in that moment was clear: secure the scene; stabilize what I could; and figure out how many patients I had and what resources were needed. The first unit on scene always assumes command. That means until backup arrives, it's on you to run the entire show, including triage, patient care, fire suppression, and resource allocation. When help gets there, you start handing off pieces of the puzzle.

But until then, it's all on your shoulders.

Joey called out from across the chaos. "LT! I see a girl! About seventy feet out. I'll go and check her out!"

"Go!" I shouted back, never breaking stride.

I kept circling the inferno, eyes scanning every angle of the burning vehicle, trying to confirm whether anyone was still trapped inside. But there was no movement. No signs of life. And if someone *had* been in there at impact, they were long gone. Nothing human could survive in that kind of fire.

It didn't burn like a normal car fire. This was something else. The speed of the flames felt like accelerants had been poured over the wreckage. Just raw fuel doing its worst.

I jogged back to Mikey. He was still locked in, hands never stopping, chest compressions steady and relentless. Anyone of my guys could run a code solo.

"Any response?" I asked.

"Nothing," he said, shaking his head.

"Alright. I'm gonna go check on Joey, then I'll send him over to back you up," I told Mikey.

From the corner of my eye, I spotted a mangled motorcycle. It had T-boned the car at a high rate of speed. The reality of what had happened began to take shape.

I looked back at the young man on whom Mikey was performing CPR, and it clicked. I needed to alert the receiving hospital's trauma team. I keyed up the mic. "Dispatch, notify the ER. I've got one adult male trauma alert. Motorcycle versus vehicle. Patient is in cardiac arrest with multiple traumatic injuries. GCS of 3. ETA ten minutes."

A few seconds passed with no response. "Dispatch, did you copy my last?" I said firmly.

She came back, sharp and clearly irritated. "I heard you. I'm trying to get a hold of them."

I get it. I know I can be a lot. I push hard. But it's not for show. It's because in this job, time isn't just important—it's everything.

Seconds matter.

When I call in a trauma alert, I need confirmation. I need to know the message got through with no guessing or delays. Because while I'm chasing radio traffic, my crew is on the street floor fighting to keep someone alive.

And I need to be right there with them. Focused. Locked in. Confident that the trauma team will be ready the moment we hit the hospital doors.

I grabbed the mic again. "Dispatch, start me an additional engine and rescue. We're still attempting to locate the driver and any possible passengers from the fully engulfed vehicle. I'll advise further."

I finally made it across the scene to Joey, who had just finished assessing the second patient.

"She's breathing," he reported, out of breath. "Banged up, but alive."

"Alright," I nodded. "Go help Mikey. I'll stay with her. Let's give that man a fighting chance."

The girl was lying on her side with her eyes locked on the man who we were working, and tears streaked down her face in shallow cries. She didn't say anything. She didn't have to. The pain in her expression said it all.

It was horrible.

In that moment, it was confirmed that they were together.

Two female officers and one male officer arrived just after we did. They were the first law enforcement on scene and a massive help. They jumped into action, immediately working to clear the growing crowd that had begun circling the wreck like moths to a flame.

"PD!" I called out.

One of them turned to me. "What can I do?"

"I need you to stay with this young woman while I try to find the missing driver from the car."

"I've got you," she said without hesitation.

I looked up, scanning the scene. Mikey was still doing CPR. Joey was securing the backboard and locking it down with practiced hands. Behind them, the car continued to rage. It was fully engulfed, and flames roared high into the air. It wasn't completely dark yet, but the fire was so intense it *felt* like night.
The flames lit the scene with a hellish glow, casting everything in flickering shadows, like a painting scorched by fire and grief.

I radioed in a full scene update for the incoming units, then turned toward the east, scanning the horizon for any sign of help.

Nothing.

No backup. No second rescue. No fire engine.

Not yet.

Eight minutes might not sound like much, but on a scene like this? It feels like thirty in hell.

The pressure in my chest was tightening. The heat burning across my back. Blood was drying on my gloves. Around us, the noise of bystanders—crying, yelling, filming—blurred into a dull, chaotic roar. My radio crackled again with more delays and more reroutes. And still, it was just us—three firefighters, two critical patients, a fully engulfed car, a missing person, possibly more, and the weight of the entire scene pressing on us.

That's when doubt started creeping in. *What am I missing? What am I doing wrong?* Every worst-case scenario flashed through my mind.

It reminded me of that moment in *Saving Private Ryan* when the explosion goes off next to Tom Hanks, and the world goes silent. Just ringing. Slow motion. Disoriented. Frozen.

Of course, the scene we were in wasn't remotely close to that level, but the *effect*, the mental fog, and the paralysis under pressure felt all too familiar.

And yet, my guys, who were barely 26 years old, were locked in. Calm. Composed. Focused. Some of the best this department has to offer. The kind of guys you'd walk through hell with and never miss a step.

Then came Mikey's voice, sharp and urgent: "LT! He's got a gun!"

The fog lifted. My focus rushed back, and I took off toward Mikey.

"PD. We've got a weapon on the patient. Please secure it!"

The officers moved without hesitation. Sure enough, there was a handgun strapped to the unconscious rider's waist. The last thing we needed was an accidental discharge while my guys were inches from his body.

I turned to one of the officers. "I need help locating the driver of that car on fire. I didn't find anyone inside, and I want to make damn sure they're not still in there—or lying somewhere nearby."

"I'm on it," he said, already running to cover the other side.

Then the officer with the young woman shouted, "Lieutenant! She's not breathing!"

I sprinted back across the scene and checked her. She was still breathing. Exhausted. But she was hanging on. Her feet were barely attached and hanging by a ligament.

"We will need to keep her awake," I told the officer. "Another rescue unit is almost here."

And then, finally, a break.

One of the officers approached at a full sprint. "LT, I found the driver. Spanish speaker."

I ran across the scene to where she stood. She was bleeding, burned, and crying. Half-hidden behind a line of onlookers, but still on her feet. Still moving.

"¿Solo usted estaba en el carro?" I asked. *Were you the only one in the car?*

Through sobs, she nodded. "Sí... solo yo."

The crowd was crying, shouting, and pleading for help. Not for themselves, but for the broken bodies lying on the pavement. It was overwhelming. Sensory overload. But her answer gave me clarity.

Finally, I could stop fixating on that burning shell and potential missing patients. No one else was inside.

We had three patients. One male in critical condition, already in cardiac arrest. One female, also critical, with altered mental status. And another female, in serious condition but still ambulatory, suffering from burns.

Just as the tension peaked, Engine 2 pulled in. Hoses came off, the crew moved fast, and they went straight to work on the fire.

One crisis down.

Then another weight was lifted. The EMS captain arrived, and I was relieved of command. Finally, I could shift my focus to our male trauma patient, still fighting for his life.

"Joey, you're at the legs. I've got the head," I said. "Lift!"

We got him onto the stretcher and into the back of the rescue.

Inside, I took a quick look around. Three of us in the back. If we were going to give this guy a real fighting chance, we needed a driver.

I keyed up the radio. "Rescue 1 to Command. I need a driver—so all three of us can work the back."

"Copy. I got one en route," Command responded.

You remember CJ from the earlier chapters. A solid firefighter, dependable under pressure. He had been fighting the car fire just moments ago, but was now reassigned to us.

He jumped in the front seat. "You ready, LT?"

"Let's go."

Joey was on CPR now. His rhythm was steady, consistent, never letting up. Mikey worked quickly, securing the IO as the needle sunk into the tibia.

"IO in. One of Epi 1:10,000 going in," Mikey called out.

"Good. Switch compressions every two minutes," I reminded them.

I took the airway.

The patient's mouth was filled with blood. Teeth were broken and scattered. I suctioned fast and deep. Then I reached for the Air-Q—a newer airway device, less invasive than a traditional ET tube but just as effective for us rescue guys.

I tried to open his mouth manually, but nothing. I needed help.

"Pass me the laryngoscope," I said. "I'll use it as a bite block to control the tongue."

Miller 5 blade. Left sweep. Careful not to displace any more teeth. I found the landmark, watched the tongue shift, and the tube slid in clean.

"Airway secure. Clear breath sounds. Let's keep moving."

The rescue rocked with every compression. The streets blurred past the windows, but none of us looked up. No one spoke unless it mattered. Every second was spent squeezing out every last ounce of hope.

Then the hospital came into view.

We pulled into the trauma bay, still working. The trauma team was already waiting—gowned up, prepped, ready to take over the moment we hit the doors. As we rolled in, the lead surgeon locked eyes with me.

"Report. Make it quick."

"Motorcycle driver T-boned a vehicle at high speed. The vehicle caught fire. Both riders were ejected. Our patient has been in full arrest since our arrival. GCS 3. CPR ongoing. IO and airway secured. Severe trauma to the head, chest, abdomen, and lower extremities."

I stepped back, soaked in sweat and blood, bunker gear still on. My boots were heavy.

My heart was heavier.

I glanced back at my guys.

Joey and Mikey stood beside me, quiet and drained, watching the trauma team take over. Their faces said everything: tired, worn down, but still dialed in. Because even after all we'd seen, even through the chaos, the blood, and the fire, we still had hope.

Hope that maybe, just maybe, this team could bring him back. That everything we gave on that street and in the truck wasn't the end of his story... but the start of a second chance.

So we stood there, shoulder to shoulder, saying nothing—just silently pulling for a miracle.

And I couldn't have been any prouder of my boys.

I'd been coordinating, communicating, and managing a chaotic scene with limited resources. But those two? They were locked in. Calm. Focused. Doing the gritty, life-saving work without hesitation and without needing direction.

That's what this job demands.

It reminded me of an incredible episode from the YouTube channel *Force TV*, featuring 104-year-old WWII Mosquito pilot Colin Bell. The interviewer asked him if he ever felt fear during missions. Bell simply said, "No, not because the danger wasn't real, but because we trained for it."

For most people, tunnel vision in a crisis leads to panic. But for those who train for it, tunnel vision becomes a cue to act. You don't freeze. You don't overthink. You default to muscle memory. There's no time for fear—just action. Your mind steps aside, and your training takes over.

But sometimes, even that isn't enough. Because reality doesn't care how hard you fight.

Just a few minutes later, the trauma surgeon walked back out. He didn't need to say a word. One look told me everything.

"The scan shows massive internal bleeding," he said. "He's gone."

...

We didn't win this one.

And it hurt. My guys were wrecked, physically and mentally. Their silence was deafening, saying more than words ever could. But they didn't fail.

We worked him from the street to the stretcher, from the stretcher to the trauma bay, without letting up for a second. We gave him every tool, every dose, and every compression.

Everything we had.

Because that's what we do.

We don't just clock in and hope for easy calls. We train. We study. We run drills when no one's watching. We carry the weight of calls like this long after the scene clears.

No matter how it ends. Good or bad.

Because out here, moments aren't measured in minutes.

They're measured in lives.

Chapter 22: Dead or Alive

I was working overtime, which is something I rarely do. Not because I've got money falling out of my pockets, but because time with my family means everything to me. Once time is gone, it's gone. However, on that day, I picked up a shift on the southeast side of the city, which is not the best area. The day had been steady with just enough calls to keep you alert. But I've always said, real danger waits for nightfall.

When midnight hits, the tones drop:

"Man down. Possible shooting."

I didn't flinch. The lights weren't as blinding this time. The tones didn't stab my ears like they used to. Familiar. Routine. Another night run. Another shooting. Another body.

It's strange what becomes "normal."

I slid into my boots, strapped in my radio, and grabbed my lid. It all felt routine—until it didn't.

I crossed the station like I'd done a thousand times, and I headed into the bay. The rescue sat quiet, peaceful even, like a jet on the deck of an aircraft carrier that is waiting for launch. All it needed was a pilot. That night, we were the pilot.

I had two firefighters riding with me, Nikki and Tony. Solid people, but not my usual crew. That meant that we'd be learning each other's rhythms on the fly. But they were sharp, and we were clicking. We lit the truck up and rolled out, the city reflecting back at us in reds and blues.

CAD notes started updating as we made our way to the scene. First it said "one victim," then "possible signal 7." PD was already on scene and had secured the area. That meant, we didn't have to stage, and we could go straight in.

But here's the thing: PD clears the scenes, but we verify patients.

Just because a cop calls it a "signal 7" (code for a dead person), doesn't mean we take their word. Their job is safety. Our role is to make sure that life isn't still hanging on by a thread.

We passed under an overpass. The engine tailed close behind with its sirens screaming, which means the call is serious but you also are getting more hands.

The street was already glowing as we approached. Cop cruisers angled like barricades. It had rained just enough to make the road slick. The kind of wet that holds heat, with steam rising like smoke from an invisible gun.

We parked with our back doors facing the scene. I stepped out and straight into a puddle.

"Of course," I muttered, shaking my head.

I snapped on my gloves, and the purple nitrile stretched tight around my wrists. I left the laptop where it sat. I needed both hands and all my focus.

PD waved us in.

There he was. One man was lying in the middle of it all. Alone. Still.

All shot up.

The worst part isn't always the blood. It's not even the body, but that scene alone can be enough to wreck your sleep. It's the aftermath.

The sound.

Screams that tear through the air like sirens. Mothers collapsing to their knees and pounding the pavement, as if they could somehow wake their child back up by force. Fathers pacing in circles, whispering prayers with clenched jaws, and trying to be strong but cracking at the edges.

And in the middle of it all—crews working, radios chirping, protocols falling into place—you're locked in. Hyper-focused on your task, but always scanning and aware.

A man stepped toward me from the edge of the crowd. He was middle-aged, with a weathered face and the look of someone who had seen more than he ever wanted to.

"Looks like he's dead," he said quietly, almost like he was talking to himself. Calm. Matter-of-fact.

I gave a quick nod, but I kept moving. I stepped past them and knelt down. Checked pulses. Nothing. But nothing isn't dead.

Not yet.

I turned to one of my guys.

"Start CPR until we can get him on the pack." Slang for LifePak monitor.

Assessing before CPR. When a patient looks obviously dead from trauma, especially in cases of violent crime like a shooting, we don't jump in blindly. Not out of laziness or callousness, but because every drop of blood, every casing, and every piece of clothing might be part of a criminal investigation. Initiating medical care could destroy crucial evidence that could help catch a killer. But there's a line. If there's even a sliver of a chance that person is still viable, we continue to fight to bring them back. We become the difference between life and death.

Because I've been doing this long enough to know that "dead" isn't always final.

We dropped the LifePak next to him, slapped on the pads, and hit the scroll wheel to "Paddles." I stared at the screen, waiting for that six-second strip to finish.

161

Flatline. Flatline.. Flatline... Flatline.... Flatline.....

Then... a bump.

A single blip of electrical activity.

Electrical vs Mechanical Activity. An electrical pulse means the heart is still firing signals, even if the muscle isn't moving. A mechanical pulse means the heart is physically contracting and creating blood flow. You can have one without the other. But electrical activity means there's still a shot, but not definitive.

I keyed up the mic: "Dispatch be advised. We're working a trauma code. Adult male with multiple gunshot wounds to the chest and face. GCS 3. ETA 10min."

Nikki dropped to compressions, and Tony prepped gear. We threw the guy on a backboard and loaded him onto the stretcher, all while keeping compressions the entire time.

We were rolling fast now. Code three. Sirens cutting through the night. I jumped to the head, where airway management is done. It was time to intubate.

What is Intubation again? Intubation is the process of inserting a breathing tube (ET tube) into the trachea to secure an airway.

The guy was bleeding heavily from his mouth and face. Bright red, fast, and relentless. I grabbed the suction and went to work with quick and aggressive passes. I knew the rule: no more than 10 seconds at a time. Any longer could tank his oxygen levels. I cleared

as much blood as I could without losing sight of the bigger goal—
airway.

I dropped in an OPA *(an oropharyngeal airway)* to keep his tongue from flopping back and closing the passage. Bagging him again, squeezing the BVM with slow, even compressions, and watching his chest rise in between chest pumps. We needed every ounce of oxygen we could push.

Then I went back in for the real thing.

This time, I grabbed my Mac blade. It was curved and familiar, and the handle was worn from years of use. I held it in my left hand, swept his tongue to the left, and started advancing. My right hand hovered, and it was ready with the tube. I leaned in, closed one eye, and focused the other eye through the blood and tissue.

I asked for cricoid pressure. One of the guys pressed just enough to bring the airway into view. No more, no less. It was a finesse move. Too much pressure, and it collapses everything. Too little pressure, and the cords disappear into the abyss.

What's Cricoid Pressure? Also known as the Sellick maneuver, is a technique where you press down on the cricoid cartilage (the ring-shaped structure just below the Adam's apple) to compress the esophagus during intubation. The idea? Prevent vomit from coming up and going down the wrong pipe while you're trying to get a tube in. It also may help to bring the vocal cords into view by stabilizing the larynx.

There it was. The epiglottis. I gently lifted, careful not to dig in or scrape teeth. Airway trauma would only make the bleeding worse.

And then I saw the tracheal rings and the black hole between them. I didn't wait. I slid the 7.5mm ET tube straight through the cords. Smooth. No hang-up. No resistance.

"I'm in," I said calmly.

I pulled back the stylet, inflated the balloon with 10cc of air, and connected the bag. I squeezed.

Right lung rise. Good.

Left lung rise. Also good.

No gurgling. No epigastric sounds. Just clean breath sounds in both lungs by auscultation, just to be sure. You don't guess on an airway.

I reached for the tube-securing device, strapped it down tight, wiped the sweat from my forehead, and looked up. My guys were already ahead of me.

They had drilled an IO right into the tibia. A clean stick. A line we could trust.

The guy's rhythm held at PEA. No pulses, but still something to work with.

Every two minutes, we paused. Checked.

Nothing.

"Resume compressions."

> **What's PEA?** *PEA stands for 'Pulseless Electrical Activity. A fancy way of saying the heart's electrical system is firing, but the muscle isn't responding. On the monitor, it might look like a normal rhythm, sinus, bradycardia, even tachycardia, but when you check for a pulse, there's nothing. Zero. It's one of the most deceptive cardiac arrests that we deal with. Looks alive on the screen, but the body's already shutting down. So we continue CPR until we can make it a shockable rhythm, a rhythm with a pulse, or they flatline—permanently.*

Fifteen minutes of CPR later, we rolled into trauma. The team was already waiting. We transferred him to the ER table, and just like that, the nurses jumped in and pounding his chest with the same urgency that we brought in from the field.

They worked him hard. Just like we did.

We stepped back, drained. The stretcher was soaked. Blood on our boots, on our gear, in the creases of our gloved hands. Our nitriles peeled off like old skin.

But I walked out with my head up. We gave him everything we had.

But eventually, they called it—

or so we thought.

A few weeks later, I was off duty, sitting at home and eating lunch when a headline stopped me cold:

"Shooting victim identifies attacker before dying."

I tapped the article without thinking. The words blurred as I read. My breath caught. A chill ran down my spine.

It was him.

It was our guy.

He had made it just long enough to speak. Just long enough to give the police a name. They arrested the shooter based on his statement.

And then… he was gone.

I set my phone down and let the silence settle around me. The kind of silence that wraps around you and doesn't let go. My whole body felt heavy with the weight of that call that had finally landed.

We didn't save his life, but we gave him enough of it back to finish something that mattered. That's why you work them. Every damn time.

Because in this life… *every second counts.*

Conclusion: Still Here

When I first started writing these stories, I didn't know what the end would look like. I just knew that these memories wouldn't leave me alone. Moments that haunted me, made me laugh, made me question things, and made me proud. I wanted to tell them right. Not polished. Not sugarcoated. Just real.

These aren't war stories that are meant to show off. They're reminders of the people that we helped, the lives that we lost, and the ones that we still carry with us. Every call in this book has left a mark on someone's life, one way or another.

But the truth is, for every chapter that I've told here, there are one thousand more that didn't make the cut. Some I won't share. Some I'll never forget, but can't explain. That's the nature of this job: *we absorb more than we ever let out.*

To the ones still riding, still working the line, still carrying the weight—*you're not alone.* Whether you're fresh out of training or thirty years in, your story matters.

I may not be the best cook in the station. I may fumble now and then. But I'll always show up. I'll always give a damn. And if nothing else, this book proves that we're more than just the calls that we run. We're human, and we've lived through some things worth telling.

So if you're still reading this, whether you're a first responder, a loved one, or just someone who wanted a glimpse into the fire rescue service, I hope it gave you something real.

We're still here. Still answering the next call.

Stay safe,

Erik Mendoza

Acknowledgments

First and foremost, I want to thank God. Thank You for always being there, for having my back, and for carrying me through. I've made my share of mistakes, but Your grace has only pushed me forward.

To my wife, Katie, thank you for your endless patience, your strength, and your love through every late night, every missed moment and bed time, and every call that stayed with me long after I came home. You've been my anchor in the chaos, and the reason I keep showing up as a better man, both on and off the job. And thank you for pouring your heart into editing this book. I know it cost you plenty of late nights, and I am endlessly grateful.

To my son, you are only two, but you've already taught me more about love, joy, and perspective than I ever thought possible. Your laughter is my reset button. Your hugs are my home. One day you'll read this, and I hope you know every word, every story, and every sacrifice was made with you in my heart.

To my expecting son, I can only imagine what you will add to our family. Your mom and I think about you every day.

To my parents, thank you for showing me what hard work, sacrifice, and unconditional love look like. Your example shaped the man that I've become. I owe so much of this journey to the foundation that you gave to me.

To my parents-in-law, thank you for welcoming me as your own and for the love and encouragement that you've shown to me along the way. Your kindness and belief in me mean more to me than you will know.

To my brothers, sisters, siblings-in-law, and all of their spouses, thank you for being my lifelong team. Your loyalty, humor, and unwavering support keep me grounded through every high and low. I'm grateful to walk this life alongside you.

To the brothers and sisters that I've had the honor of riding with, this book is just as much yours as it is mine. Every call, every laugh, and every quiet moment in between shaped these stories. I may be the one at the keyboard, but we lived these times together.

To my mentors, officers, and senior guys who showed me how to do the job the right way, even when no one was watching, thank you. Your lessons echo in every page.

To the young guys coming up: *Keep showing up. Keep learning. Keep caring.* One day, you'll have your own stories, and they'll matter more than you realize.

To the reader: whether you're in the fire service or not, thank you for picking this book. If it made you feel something. If it brought a little understanding, laughter, or even healing, then it did its job.

To the ones we've lost, may your memory live on through the stories that we continue to tell.

God bless always.

Definitions and Firehouse Slang

Altered Mental Status: A general term describing a patient who is not thinking clearly or acting normally. This can range from confusion to unconsciousness and may be caused by trauma, illness, drugs, or lack of oxygen.

Auscultation: Listening to internal body sounds, such as heart or lung sounds, using a stethoscope.

Avulsion: A traumatic injury where skin or tissue is torn away from the body.

Backboard: A rigid board used to immobilize a patient's spine during movement, especially when spinal injury is suspected.

Bag Valve Mask: A handheld device used to manually provide oxygen and ventilation to a patient who is not breathing adequately.

Bagged: Slang for manually ventilating a patient using a bag valve mask.

Bay: The garage area of a fire station where apparatus are parked.

Blow By Oxygen: Delivering oxygen near a patient's face without a mask, commonly used for children or patients who cannot tolerate direct application.

Bunked Out: Fully dressed in firefighting protective gear, ready for action.

Cervical Collar: A rigid brace placed around the neck to immobilize the cervical spine and prevent further injury.

Charlie Side: Fire ground terminology referring to the rear side of a structure, opposite the front or Alpha side.

C Spine: Short for cervical spine. Refers to the neck portion of the spinal column.

Cutters: Hydraulic rescue tools designed to cut through metal, commonly used during vehicle extrications.

Driver Engineer: The firefighter responsible for driving the apparatus and operating the pump and onboard equipment.

Extricated: Safely removed from a vehicle or confined space, often using specialized rescue tools.

Fire Engine: A fire apparatus primarily equipped for firefighting operations, including hoses, water, pumps, and basic rescue equipment.

GCS: Glasgow Coma Scale. A neurological scoring system used to assess a patient's level of consciousness based on eye, verbal, and motor responses.

Get Me Some Ears: Slang request for a stethoscope, typically shouted during a chaotic medical scene.

GSW: Gunshot wound.

Hydraulic Ram: A rescue tool used to push or spread parts of a vehicle apart during extrication.

Hypoglycemia: A condition where blood sugar levels drop too low, often causing confusion, sweating, seizures, or loss of consciousness.

IV: Intravenous access used to deliver fluids or medications directly into a patient's bloodstream.

Joules: A unit of energy used to measure the amount of electricity delivered during defibrillation or cardioversion.

Leads: Electrodes placed on a patient's body to monitor heart rhythms on a cardiac monitor.

Life Pack: A portable cardiac monitor and defibrillator used by EMS to assess heart rhythms, deliver shocks, and monitor vital signs.

Level 1 Trauma: The highest designation for trauma centers, equipped to handle the most severe and complex injuries.

Lt: Short for Lieutenant. A fire officer who supervises a crew and manages operations on scene.

New York Hook: A long metal tool used for forcible entry, overhaul, and pulling down ceilings or walls during fire operations.

Non-Rebreather Mask: An oxygen mask capable of delivering high concentrations of oxygen using a reservoir bag.

Overhaul: The process of searching for and extinguishing hidden fire after the main fire has been knocked down.

PD: Police Department.

Pneumothorax: A collapsed lung caused by air entering the space between the lung and chest wall, often due to trauma.

Probies: New firefighters still in their probationary period, learning the job and earning their place in the firehouse.

Purple Nitrile: Protective medical gloves worn by firefighters and paramedics during patient care.

Rescue Truck: An apparatus equipped with advanced medical equipment, and personnel trained for both fire and EMS.

Saline Lock: An IV line placed without continuous fluids, allowing quick medication administration if needed.

Signal 7: A radio code used to indicate a confirmed death.

Spreaders: Hydraulic rescue tools used to pry open doors, dashboards, or metal structures during extrication.

The Box: Slang for the ambulance or rescue unit where patient care and transport occur.

Throw in a Line: Fire ground slang meaning to start an IV.